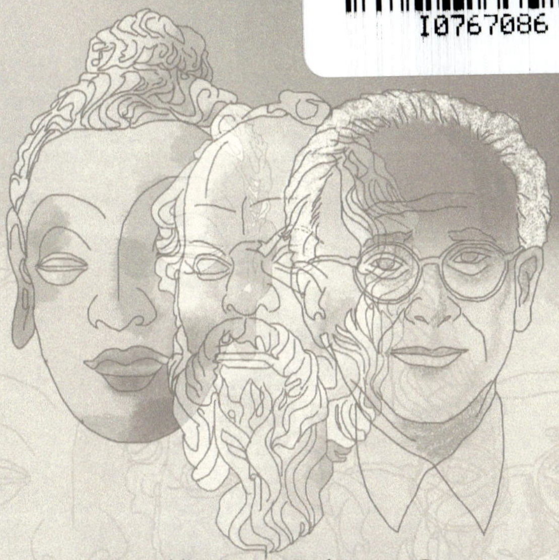

The Buddha, Socrates and Antonio Damasio

Buddha to Damasio

ETHICAL THOUGHT

Venkata Mohan

Buddha to Damasio

Ethical Thought

Venkata Mohan

Notion Press

Old No. 38, New No. 6
McNichols Road, Chetpet
Chennai - 600 031

First Published by Notion Press 2017
Copyright © Venkata Mohan 2017
All Rights Reserved.

Hardcase ISBN: 979-8-89519-090-6
Paperback ISBN: 978-1-94749-870-9

Cartoons and cover design by : Ramana Jeevi

PREFACE

Why is a certain behavior considered ethical? By what processes does a certain behavior become ethical? Why are some people more capable of behaving ethically? This book discusses questions such as these with the help of the perspectives drawn from three distinct fields: Religion, Philosophy and Neuroscience. Theorists from the ancient to the recent – the Buddha and Socrates to Antonio Damasio – are covered.

In a way, this book is an extension of my *Sociological Thought: In the Light of J. Krishnamurti's Philosophy* (2010). I would like to suggest to the readers that they also go through the ethics-related topics from that book – Karl Marx, Hegel, Herbert Spencer, Robert Michels, Kant, Schopenhauer, Nietzsche, Freud, Reflections on Social Order, Ayn Rand, J. Krishnamurti, and Osho and his Krishna.

Venkata Mohan

Contents

1. Socrates

Historical situation

Athens was a city-state that had democracy as early as the 5th century BC. That democracy was not like ours where only representatives are sent to the assembly. In Athens all the voters were members of the assembly. Theirs was a *direct democracy*; ours is a *representative democracy*.

In their direct democracy, however, slaves and women didn't have votes. Of a population of 400,000 around 250,000 were slaves! Surely not all the eligible might be active in the assembly.

Athens had its golden period during the rule of Pericles. It had a big navy. It developed trade with island states. Pericles built huge buildings. Parthenon, the chief temple dedicated to the goddess Athena, was perhaps the most imitated building in the world.

The golden age, however, was over when Athens got involved in a war with Sparta, a great power at that time but having an authoritarian regime. This war broke out in 431 BC. Pericles died in the second year of the war, when a plague broke out. Pericles was not succeeded by any great ruler. And a series of military disasters for which the democratic government was responsible led to Athens' utter defeat and its subsequent surrender in 404 BC. Thucydides' account of this war as given in his *Peloponnesian War* is still a standard text in military planning as well as International Relations!

Soon after the defeat in the war, aristocrats abolished democracy and ruled for some time against the will of the people. Plato's family was part of that aristocracy. Finally their rule was replaced by democracy.

It was not aristocracy but democracy that put one of the world's greatest philosophers, Socrates, on trial. At the end of the trial, Socrates was asked to drink hemlock, which he did. This took place in 399 BC. He was seventy years old then.

Plato (427– 347 BC) was born in Athens. He was growing up during the Peloponnesian War that Thucydides was writing about. Plato had studied under Socrates for eight years. He was a witness to his master's trial and was profoundly moved by the state's sentencing of wisdom to death.

Plato on Socrates' death

[Plato wrote the following in his *Phaedo*]

"Then, holding the cup to his lips, quite readily and cheerfully he drank the poison. And hitherto most of us had been able to control our sorrow; but now when we saw him drinking, and saw that he had finished the draught, we could no longer forbear, and in spite of myself, my own tears were flowing fast; so that I covered my face and wept over myself; for themselves.

2. Some may say this is too rational an approach to life; in reality, man is irrational; motives play a role and the unconscious shapes the behavior. That is not denied. But how is Freud healing his patients? The aim of psychoanalysis is to help the patients see for themselves the causes and the consequences of their problems. That is to make them knowledgeable about themselves.

3. Even if a man is helplessly trapped by evil, knowledge is the way to get him out of it. It is a different matter that such knowledge may not be communicated verbally.

4. If Socrates' statement is not acceptable, it may be because people equate knowledge with the ability to talk about it or write about it. But to Socrates, knowledge is deeper understanding – only that contributes to virtue.

5. In saying 'virtue is knowledge', Socrates is not only right but kind towards human beings and tolerant of their vulnerabilities.

6. Surely Socrates is referring to some of the basic forms of virtue like not stealing, not deceiving, not harming anyone knowingly, and repaying debts. He is not suggesting that whatever is considered good in public opinion is a virtue. Though condemned to die, Socrates thought of himself – as his disciples agreed – that he was being virtuous.

Evaluation B

1. In *The Republic*, virtue in general is discussed. Accommodation of contrary views would have been possible if specific virtues had been taken into

consideration. The view of Thrasymachus that laws serve to protect the interests of the powerful (which Marx takes up) or the view of Protagoras that morality is based on conventions specific to cultures (which is what Anthropology propounds) can be accommodated by delving into the specifics.

2. Anyway, the latter-day critics of Plato took cues from the critics of Plato in *The Republic,* some of whom were called *sophists.* The history of thought thus followed the method of dialectics – evolution of the higher truth through the resolution of contradictions.

♦ ♦ ♦

Jesus: The un-virtuous will go to hell.

Socrates: Please don't say that. They are only ignorant people.

Questions to think about

1. To which city state did Socrates belong? Was it a direct democracy?

2. Did his city state believe in political equality?

3. What do you know about Pericles?

4. How was Sparta different from Athens?

5. What were the causes of the Peloponnesian war? When did it take place?

6. What do you know about Thucydides?

7. What was the nature of government at the time of Socrates's death?

8. When was Socrates born? When did he die?

9. What is Plato's relationship with Socrates?

10. What are our sources to learn about Socrates's philosophy?

11. What is the Socratic method?

12. On what grounds was Socrates charged?

13. What do you know about trial of Socrates?

14. Why did Socrates choose to die?

15. Did Socrates think the state was justified in sentencing him? Why did he not think of escaping?

16. Do you think he should have escaped and contributed more to Philosophy?

17. Analyse these Socratic positions

   - "No one does evil voluntarily"

- "Unexamined life is not worth living."
- "Virtue is knowledge."

18. What is meant by unity between knowledge, happiness and virtue?

19. Why do some people choose to be dishonest to be happy? What would Socrates say on this matter? Do you agree with him?

20. Who is a better person between happy but dishonest and unhappy but honest?

21. What is meant by integrity?

22. In 'Virtue is knowledge' what is the virtue that Socrates is referring to?

23. If a person is happy being corrupt and another happy being honest, whose happiness is of a higher value? On what basis? On the basis of intensity? Or duration? Or something else?

24. How is 'virtue is knowledge' different from 'knowledge is virtue'?

25. Is knowledge enough for one to be virtuous?

26. What is meant by happiness? Does Socrates define happiness differently?

27. What do you think is the main limitation in the Socratic method of transformation?

28. Why do many people resist self-introspection?

29. What advantages does self-introspection give one?

30. Compare Socrates with Gandhi.

2. Plato

Tripartite soul

What is that knowledge of oneself that makes one virtuous?

According to Plato, the human soul has three elements or three parts. If one doesn't like the word soul, one may substitute it with personality – which Freud did.

One element is *body appetite*, which deals with the physical needs and pleasures. That part is clear. Another element is *spirit*. This deals with aggression, pride, loyalty, or courage. What does one make of this? Plato is referring to the psychological element as opposed to the physiological element covered under body appetite. The third element is *reason* which can guide the individual and enable him to know truth.

To Plato, justice of a soul is in maintaining harmony among these three elements. It doesn't mean giving equal importance to all the three elements, but knowing their relative roles and their relative importance. Body appetite is the lowest level element; spirit belongs to the intermediate level, and reason belongs to the highest level. Both body appetite and spirit have their own importance but they should be guided by reason. Only such an arrangement brings justice to the soul. Only that gives happiness. Living in such harmony makes man virtuous as well as happy. There is no conflict between being virtuous and being happy.

Therefore, pursuing pleasure without regard to spirit or reason will lead to unhappiness. Plato thus thought that both physiological needs and psychological needs should be guided by reason. Interestingly, Freud chose to divide personality in a way different from Plato's. *Id* deals with the instincts – sex and aggression. It goes by the *pleasure principle*. *Superego* covers the morals. And *Ego* tries to mediate between the two elements and works as per the *reality principle*. Individual and social elements are to be guided by reason, in Freud's scheme.

Common to Plato and Freud is the point that there should be harmony among these three elements. Harmony brings happiness, and disharmony sorrow.

Ideal state

Plato believes that individuals differ in terms of the element that dominates in them: body appetite in some, spirit in some, and reason in some. These differences are partly inherited and partly the result of upbringing.

Plato wants to use these individual differences to create a just society. The people with dominance of body appetite should make up *producer class*. Those with the dominance of spirit should make up *military class*. These two classes should be led by reason-dominant individuals that make up the *guardian class*.

Those who are to be a part of the guardian class will be identified early and brought up differently. They are to be trained in dialectics. Since the reason-dominance is partly a matter of inheritance, a superior man will be allowed to mate with only a superior woman so that superior children may be born. But the partners will not be told that they are teamed as per the reason-dominance. They will be given the impression that they have been chosen randomly. And if inferior children are born, they will be left to die! So guardians will not be allowed to have sex as they wish. Nor can they have a family or own any property. But the other two classes can lead less restrictive lives. All this he writes in *The Republic* (which in those days meant justice, unlike its current meaning of electing the highest authority).

To Plato, a city is a man "writ large against the sky". What is true of an individual is true of a society. What is a desirable relationship among the elements within an individual is also a desirable relationship among classes in a city-state.

Thankfully, no society has sought the assistance of Plato – despite his efforts – in organizing itself.

Evaluation

1. What Plato fails to see is that harmony can only come voluntarily, and it can never be forced, either on an individual or a society.

2. During his trial, Socrates said that he was surprised when he heard that an oracle had said that he was the wisest of all men. Socrates wanted to find out why that oracle had said so. He met political leaders, writers, and

poets to know how they might not be wiser than him. Then he concluded that the oracle had called him the wisest because he only knew that he really didn't know anything important! Given such an attitude, Socrates would surely have disapproved of Plato's master plans for social engineering.

3. The theory of individual differences has certain interesting applications. If a body-appetite-dominant person is placed in a reason-dominant position, it creates ground for an unjust soul as well as an unjust society!

Allegory of Cave

Plato seems to believe that immutable truth is knowable through reason and the method of dialectic. It is this conviction that is behind his audacious plans.

Through an allegory of cave, Plato points out the difficulty in explaining the reality to those who never saw it. In a cave four prisoners are kept chained. They can't even turn back their heads. Behind them there is a fire. Between the fire and the men there is a path on which different objects and people are moving and as they move, their shadows fall on the wall of the cave. The prisoners can only see the shadows. They can see neither the real objects nor the fire that is creating the shadows of the real on the wall.

One prisoner is then released. He goes out and sees the fire, the moving objects, and learns how shadows are created and how they are distorted from the real figures. He goes into the cave to explain it all to his former prison-mates. But they can't make anything of what he is saying.

All through the centuries, philosophers have tried to figure out what this allegory means. The allegory suggests that Plato believes that one can come out of the cave and see the truth completely.

Evaluation

1. The one who comes out of the cave and sees how the shadows are being formed on the wall of the cave knows the truth that is at a higher level than that of those who are still chained in the cave. But that doesn't mean his truth is ultimate.

2. Truth is relative. A higher level truth can explain successfully something below it. But it can't claim absoluteness.

3. This issue is settled, once for all, by Kant. He showed how reality is limited and distorted as it is revealed through human faculties – senses and mind included. No claims on the absolute should henceforth be made by any philosopher – it is decreed.

On philosopher kings

Plato believes that ideally those who saw the truth – that is, those who got out of the cave – should rule. "Until philosophers become kings in this world or those whom we call kings and rulers really and truly become philosophers, and political power and philosophy thus come into the same hands… there is no other road to happiness, either for society or individual." To Plato, democracy is not the best form of government.

Plato: Some can get out of the cave and see the truth.

Kant: They can get out of a small cave only to enter a bigger one.

♦ ♦ ♦

Questions to think about

1. What is meant by harmony within an individual?

2. What is meant by justice of soul?

3. What is an ideal state?

4. What do you know about producer class, military class and guardian class?

5. How is city a man "writ large against the sky?"

6. What is the concept of philosopher-king?

7. What does the allegory of cave represent?

8. Discuss why democracy may not be able to elect the best.

3. Aristotle

Aristotle (384–322 BC) was born in Stagira, a city in Macedonia. His father was a physician in the king's court. He came to Athens to study and became a favorite pupil of Plato for 20 years. He left Athens only after Plato's death. He came back again to set up his school, the Lyceum. This school was devoted more to biology and natural sciences whereas The Academy that Plato left was devoted more to mathematics and political philosophy. Before that, he had become a tutor to Alexander the Great in 343 BC, who later financed and organized Aristotle's collection of various manuscripts and biological specimens. Athens that came under the Macedonian empire in 338 BC turned hostile to Aristotle. So he left the city after Alexander's death in 323 BC.

Aristotle's knowledge was very, very wide. He was a pioneer in systematizing and developing many branches of knowledge: biology, physics, logic, aesthetics, politics and philosophy. While Plato was imaginative and idealistic, Aristotle was pragmatic and empirical in approach. He compared 150 constitutions of the

Greek states, for example.

Aristotle's views on ethics are mentioned in *Nicomachean ethics*, which was a compilation of his lecture notes, not written for publication. He agrees with Plato that adherence to traditional virtues brings happiness. He doesn't deviate from the position that virtue is knowledge.

Intellect being the chief characteristic feature of man, Aristotle holds that exercise of the intellect gives man the greatest of happiness. This is called the *essentialist argument*.

He advances the *doctrine of the mean* in managing emotions. The mean doesn't refer to the available extremes of outside things. It refers to feelings. Courage is the mean between cowardice and recklessness, temperance between abstinence and self-indulgence and proper pride between vanity and humility. Of course something like truthfulness did not fit into this scheme.

Aristotle believes that no emotion by itself is wrong. It is all about showing the right emotion at the right time, on the right grounds, towards the right people and in the right way. But how does one feel rightly and express rightly? This is the function of reason, which enables man to be in touch with reality.

Aristotle criticized the extremes that Plato advocated in creating an ideal state. Aristotle was against destruction of the private sphere. There should be family, not community of wives that Plato proposed. "What is common to the greatest number gets the least amount of care." He is not for the abolition of private property. "Those who work more and get less recompense are bound to raise complaints." Aristotle thinks participation of the people is important in itself, and the idea of philosopher-king is not appropriate. Given the restrictions imposed on the guardian class, Aristotle says the class wouldn't be happy that way.

In all this one can see Aristotle is pragmatic and that his idea of human nature is closer to empirical reality.

Plato: *Justice is harmony among the parts – be they of an individual or a city state*

Aristotle: True, but that harmony can't be imposed from above.

♦ ♦ ♦

Justice as fit

Plato thought that each class should be made up of people with appropriate predisposition. Only then would there be harmony within an individual and harmony within the state. This harmony is justice, and this is happiness. Aristotle agrees with the idea that justice lies in keeping right people at the right place.

Aristotle thinks people are different and each one should try to realize his essential nature. Happiness lies in the realization of one's essence.

What Aristotle thought might look obvious, but it is not so. Our education tried to convey to us the idea that people are equal and similar and each one should try to reach the highest level possible in a social hierarchy. A better system creates equal opportunities to reach the top.

But Aristotle's view is that people are different and a system is good and just when it succeeds in placing people in the positions that match with their nature. Justice does not mean equal opportunity for all to reach the top, but realization of one's essence – the difference with others!

Controversially, Aristotle said some would be better off being slaves, though he did not say that the slaves in his society were better off being slaves.

What should be the nature of recruitment the positions of authority? One should consider what qualities that position requires and accordingly select the candidate. Candidates will be happy and the system will do what it is expected to do.

Evaluation

1. There is a lot that the current education system has to learn from Aristotle's views. This is forcing everyone to achieve and achieve, with no attention paid to the learner's aptitude.

2. The idea of differences is exaggerated. People often value the same things. They fight over the same things. The

idea that some people should only be slaves does grave injustice to human nature.

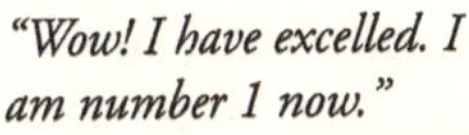

♦ ♦ ♦

Questions to think about

1. Is essence the same thing as ability?

2. How should the state recruit people to various posts based on the essence?

3. What is meant by honesty?

4. What is a just state?

5. What is meant by essentialist argument?

6. Did Aristotle agree with Plato's ideal state? Explain.

7. If we have to distribute a limited number of flutes among a large group of students, how should we go about it?

8. To whom should we give priority on a tennis court – to two good players, or two scientists who want to relax?

9. Casey Martin was a professional golfer with a bad leg. He requested the association to permit him to use a golf cart during the tournament. Should his request be granted?

10. What is the relevance of Aristotle to the designing of the education system?

11. What is meant by the following:

    - "Justice is giving each person his due."

    - "Any polis which is truly so called must devote itself to the end of encouraging goodness."

◆ ◆ ◆

4. Thucydides

The conversations given below are taken from *History of the Peloponnesian War* written by Thucydides. They reveal what the Athenians thought about power and its relationship with justice during the Peloponnesian War fought between Athens and Sparta. The war which was witnessed by Thucydides broke out in 431 BC and lasted for 27 years.

Currently, those who belong to the school of 'Realism' in International Relations share the Athenians' attitude towards power.

Melian Dialogue

This gives an account of the dialogue between the people of Melos, a small island in the Aegean Sea, and the Athenians in 416-5 BC. Melos was a neutral island. The Athenians wanted to conquer it. They demanded that Melos join the Delian League and become a part of their empire. The Athenians put forward their demand for 'surrender or face destruction' before the Melian council.

Athenians: We on our side will use no fine phrases saying, for example, that we have a right to our empire because we defeated the Persians, or that we have come against you now because we defeated the Persians, or that we have come against you now because of the injuries you have caused us – a great mass of words that nobody would believe.

And we ask you not to imagine that you will influence us by saying that you, despite being a colony of Sparta, have not joined Sparta in the war, or that you have never done us any harm.

We recommend that you should try to get what is possible for you to get, taking into consideration what we both really do think. You know as well as we do that when these matters are discussed by practical people, the standard of justice depends on the equality of power to compel and that in fact the strong do what they have the power to do and the weak accept what they have to accept.

By giving in you would be able to save yourselves from disaster. And we, by not destroying you, would be able to profit from you.

Melians: So you would not agree to our being neutral, friends instead of enemies, but allies of neither side?

Athenians: No, because it is not so much your hostility that worries us. Rather the case is that, if we were on friendly terms with you, our subjects would take that as a sign of weakness in us, whereas your hatred is evidence of our power.

Melians: Is that your subjects' idea of fair play? That no distinction should be made between people who are quite unconnected with you and people who are mostly your own colonists or else rebels whom you have conquered?

Athenians: So far as right and wrong are concerned they think that there is no difference between the two, that those who still preserve their independence do so because they are strong, and that if we fail to attack them, it is because we are afraid. We rule the sea and you are islanders, weaker islanders than the others. It is therefore particularly important that you should not escape.

Melians: Do you think that there is no security for you in what we suggest? Since you will not let us mention justice but tell us to give in to your interests, we too must tell you what our interests are and , if yours and ours happen to coincide, we must try to persuade you of the fact. Is it not certain that you will make enemies of all states who are at present neutral, when they see what is happening here and naturally conclude that in course of time you will attack them too? Does not this mean that you are strengthening the enemies you already have and are forcing others to become your enemies even against their intentions and inclinations?

Athenians: As a matter of fact, we are not so much frightened of the states on the continent. They have their liberty and this means that it will be a long time before they begin to take precautions against us. We are more concerned about islanders like yourselves, who are still unsubdued or subjects who have already become embittered by the constraint which our empire imposes on them. These are the people who are most likely to act in a reckless manner and bring themselves and us, too, into the most obvious danger.

Melians: Then surely, if such hazards are taken by you to keep your empire and by your subjects to escape from it, we who are still free would show ourselves great cowards and weaklings if we failed to face everything that comes rather than submit to slavery.

Athenians: No, not if you are sensible. This is no fair fight, with honor on one side and shame on the other. It is a question of saving your lives and not resisting those who are far too strong for you.

Melians: Yet we know that in war fortune sometimes makes the odds more level than could be expected from the difference in numbers of the two sides. And if we surrender, then all our hope is lost at once, whereas, as long as we remain in action, there is still a hope that we may yet stand upright.

Athenians: Hope, that comforter in danger. If one has solid advantage to fall back upon, one can indulge in hope. It may do harm, but will not destroy one. But hope is by nature an expensive commodity, and those who are risking their all on one cast find out what it means only when they are already ruined. Do not be like those people who miss the chance of saving themselves in a human and practical way and turn to prophecies and oracles and other such things which by encouraging hope lead men to ruin.

Melians: Nevertheless we trust that the gods will give us fortune as good as yours because we are standing for what is right against what is wrong.

For what we lack in power, we trust that it will be made up for by our alliance with the Spartans, who are bound, if for no other reason than for honor's sake, and because we are their kinsmen, to come to our help. Our confidence is not so irrational as you think.

Athenians: So far as the favor of the gods is concerned, we think we have as much right to that as you have. Our aims and our actions are perfectly consistent with the beliefs men hold about the gods and with the principles which govern their own conduct. Our opinion of the gods and our knowledge of men lead us to conclude that it is a general and necessary law of nature to rule whatever one can. This is not a law that we have made, nor were we the first to act upon it when it was made. We found that it already existed, and we shall leave it to exist for ever among those who come after us. We are merely acting in accordance with it, and we know that you or anybody else with the same power as ours would be acting in precisely the same way. And therefore, so far as the gods are concerned, we see no good reason why we should fear to be at a disadvantage.

With regard to your views about Sparta and your confidence that she, out of a sense of honor, will come to your aid, we must say that we congratulate you on your naivete but do not envy you your folly. In matters that concern themselves or their own constitution the Spartans are remarkably good. As for their relations with others, that is a long story. But it can be expressed shortly and clearly by saying that of all the people we know the Spartans are most conspicuous for believing that what they like doing is honorable and what suits their interest is just.

When you are allowed to choose between war and safety, you will not be so insensitively arrogant as to make the wrong choice. This is the safe rule – to stand up to one's equals, to

Athenians to Melians: *God made the law that the strong should crush the weak, and we are only implementing His law.*

behave with deference towards one's superiors, and to treat one's inferiors with moderation.

Ultimately the Melians refused to surrender. Consequently, war followed. Eventually the Athenians won. They put to death all the men of military age whom they had captured and sold the women and children as slaves and repopulated Melos as an Athenian colony.

Mytilenian Debate

Mytilene was one of the non-tributary members of the Delian League. It feared that it would be reduced to a tributary member and so started preparation to rebel against Athene with the assistance of the Spartans. The Athenians wanted to crush the Mytilenians before they could equip themselves to rebel.

Mytilene was an oligarchy. Some Mytilenians, known as proxenoi, were sympathetic to democracy. They alerted the Athenians who invaded Mytilene that was unprepared for war.

The Athenian assembly, scared of further revolts, hastily sentenced all the male citizens of Mytilene to death, and sold the women and children into slavery. A trireme was dispatched to Mytilene and it slaughtered all the prisoners, numbering around a thousand. The next day, the Athenians realized the brutality of their actions and wanted to reconsider the decision to massacre all the men instead of just the guilty. In the debate, Cleon argues in favour of massacre, and Diodotus against it. The assembly accepts Diodotus' position and only prominent l eaders of the revolt were executed. This Mytilenian debate took place in 427 BC.

Cleon's argument

Personally I have had occasion often enough already to observe that a democracy is incapable of governing others, and I am all the more convinced of this when I see how you are now changing your minds about the Mytilenians.

Because fear and conspiracy play a part in your daily relations with each other, you imagine that the same thing is true of your allies.

You fail to see that when you allow them to persuade you to make a mistaken decision and when you give way to your own feelings of compassion you are being guilty of a kind of weakness which is dangerous to you and which will not make them love you anymore. What you don't realize is that your empire is a tyranny exercised over subjects who do not like it and who are always plotting against you. You will not make them obey you by harming your own interests in order to do them a favor. Your leadership depends on superior strength and not on their goodwill.

You propose to hold power. Then your interests demand that they be punished. The only alternative is to surrender your empire, so that you may afford to go in for philanthropy.

Punish them as they deserve and thereby set an example to your other allies to show that any revolt will be punished by death.

Diodotus responds

If we are sensible people, we shall see that th e question is not so much whether they are guilty as whether we are making the right decision for ourselves. I might prove that they are the most guilty people in the world, but it does not follow that I shall propose the death penalty, unless that is in your interests. I might argue that they deserve to be forgiven, but should not recommend forgiveness unless that seems to me the best thing for the state.

It is not a law court where we have to consider what is fit and just. It is a political assembly, and the question is how Mytilene can be most useful to Athens.

If a city has revolted and realizes that the revolt can't succeed, it will come to terms while it is still capable of paying an indemnity and continuing to pay tribute afterwards. But if Cleon's method is adopted, can you not see that every city will not only make much more careful preparations for revolt, but will also hold out against siege to the very end, since to surrender early or late means just the same thing? This is unquestionably against our interests – to spend money on a siege because of the impossibility of coming to terms, and, if we capture the place, to take over a city that is in ruins so that we lose the future revenue from it. And it is just on this revenue that our strength in war depends.

The right way to deal with free people is this – not to inflict tremendous punishments on them after they have revolted, but to take tremendous care of them before this point is reached, to prevent them from even contemplating the idea of revolt, and, if we do have to use force against them, to hold as few as possible of them responsible for this.

Do not be swayed too much by pity or by ordinary decent feelings. I, no less than Cleon, wish you to be influenced by such emotions.

◆ ◆ ◆

Questions to think about

1. What do you know about the context of Thucydides's work?

2. Give salient points of Melians and Athenians during the Melian Dialogue.

3. Did the Melians make the right choice?

4. Give the salient points raised by the speakers during the Mytilenian Debate.

5. Is the other's power a source of threat to one?

6. Does power influence the notions of justice?

7. Are justice and power one and the same? Or is power a factor of justice?

8. Does power play a role between individuals within a society?

9. Is what is considered ethical between members of a society ethical between two nations also?

10. Can there be anything ethical in the conduct of international relations?

11. What is meant by the 'interest' of a nation?

12. Should an administrator give importance to power or only to the rules?

5. David Hume

David Hume (1711-76) got the impression – rightly or wrongly – that those who proposed reason as the basis of morality missed the role of passions. In response to such a view, Hume showed how passions are the basis of morality and not reason. In this process of proving the role of passions, as opposed to reason, Hume indeed arrived at an ingenious way of looking at morality.

In the context of the history of ideas, Hume belongs to the empiricist tradition of the *Age of Enlightenment* (1650-1770). This tradition which Hume shares with John Locke (1632-1704) was opposed to the rationalist tradition of Plato and Descartes (1596-1650).

Hume said logic and mathematics deal with *relations of ideas*. These propositions have certainty, following from a set of assumptions. But there are some propositions that state *matters of fact*, Hume said. Such propositions can never be certain. "The sun rises every day" is true as long as the sun rises and it may not rise tomorrow. There is no law that it should rise. Of course we can go around our lives assuming that what has been happening all these centuries will happen tomorrow too.

Hume said that matters of fact that don't have any basis in sensory experience should be rejected. So he rejected the idea of God, and the idea of soul since they do not have corresponding sensory experiences.

He rejected 'self' too, which he said is imagined continuity whereas what an individual experiences is only a series of sensations. (Interestingly, realizing this unreality of self is the cherished goal in Hinduism and Buddhism!)

How can morality be explained through sensory experiences? In fact, Hume was shocked when he first read Francis Hutcheson, a moral philosopher, who said that morality was based neither on the Bible as Christians believed, nor on reason as Socrates said, but on the sentiments of approval and disapproval. That was how he started working on the validity of the sensations in the generation of correct knowledge. Hume's theory of morality is part of his empiricism. His theory is given in *Enquiry Concerning the Principles of Morals* (1751). Let us see how he explains morality in terms of sensations.

Suppose 'A', 'B' and 'C' are on an island. Suppose 'B' did something to hurt 'C'. Then 'C' feels unpleasant. What makes one feel unpleasant may or may not be moral. Then 'C' tells 'A' what 'B' did to him. Suppose 'A' places himself in the position of 'C' and also feels unpleasant. Why does 'A' also feel unpleasant, though nothing has been done to him? Well, that is human nature. That is what we are born with. That fellow feeling – let us call it *sympathy* – is part of inherited make-up. Hume is not saying we should cultivate it. He is not saying that it is a virtue.

He is saying that is what it is. It is basic and fundamental to human existence. That is the source of all the virtues!

So when 'C' feels bad and 'A' also feels bad, something about what is bad is arrived at. Pleasantness and unpleasantness determine what is good and what is bad.

When is something a virtue? It should be pleasant to the possessor or the others or both. What is a vice? It should cause unpleasantness to the possessor or to the others or both. Note that Hume is introducing three criteria – either for oneself, or for the others, or for both. Trust is a virtue because it is good for the others. Politeness is a virtue because it is good for the others. Tranquility is a virtue because it is good for oneself as well as for the others.

Why then did he not say that whatever is pleasant to oneself is moral? Why is morality defined differently from pleasure? Morality involves a judgment without reference to any specific person. Rules are pleasure-based, but are person-neutral.

When a woman says 'my husband hurt me,' she is stating her problem. But when she says 'what he did is immoral,' she is inviting others' support. She can't get others' support unless her grievance is at a level that others too feel the way she feels. When others too feel similarly, her husband's behavior gets the label 'immoral'.

So sensations are felt at an individual level. Sympathy enables one to feel for the other. For such sympathy to touch diverse people, the cause of the pain should be at a level that can be termed immoral.

Hume says, sometimes one also asks 'if everyone does this, can society survive?' For something to acquire the status of a moral principle, it has to pass through the scrutiny of higher standards.

Evaluation A

1. Surely an interesting way of looking at. This theory gives an insight that Plato's does not.

2. But it would be wrong to say Hume's theory demolishes Plato's. It can't be said that the reason-based theories stand demolished and the passion-based explanations validated. Why do we say this?

    The idea that reason is ever proposed in opposition to passion is not correct. The point is that passions are many. They are conflicting. They work at cross purposes. Some passions demand immediate satisfaction but yielding to them may bring big trouble. Reason is supposed to assess this play of passions. Reason is supposed to assist the realization of passions on a long-term basis. That is what happiness is. So reason was not meant to tame passions, but to realize them in a harmonious way.

3. 'No one does evil voluntarily' means no one forgoes happiness knowingly. Socrates is only banking on man's desire for continuous, uninterrupted sensations of positive feelings – one word for that is happiness. Socrates finds out that one such condition for being happy is to be ethical!

Evaluation B

Hume's theory has important implications for pathological forms of immoral behavior.

Morality is based on the working of sympathy. Continuing the example, 'A' feels the pain of 'C'. It means he feels the pain of the other, though he is not directly wounded. Suppose this ability of 'A' is damaged!

Second, 'A' wants 'C' to be out of pain. Because 'A' himself wants to be out of a similar situation, out of pain. Suppose this ability of 'A' is damaged!

Hume didn't assume unnatural things. But when these natural things are damaged through faulty upbringing, the ground for immoral as well as self-destructive behavior is laid.

Evaluation C

What happens to ethics in the era of globalization? The general standards are likely to be much broader, more fundamental and less constrained by narrowness of specific cultures. More humane societies will result. We can see this growing range of issues being discussed under human rights, for example.

Why do even the progressive thinkers of the past appear to be holding very illiberal views? They are being evaluated by the present which is a product of advanced ethics.

The *Age of Enlightenment* itself is a result of exposure to new ideas and cultures of the past as well as the contemporary but distant.

A quote from Hume

On sympathy, he said "Though this affection of humanity may not generally be esteemed so strong as vanity or ambition, yet, being common to all men, it alone can be the foundation of morals or of any general system of blame or praise."

◆ ◆ ◆

Questions to think about

1. What do you know about the Age of Enlightenment?

2. How, according to Hume, does something become ethical?

3. When is kindness more effective? Or is it equally effective everywhere?

4. What, according to Socrates/Plato/Aristotle, becomes ethical?

5. What is empiricism? How is it different from rationalism?

6. Is sympathy inherent in human beings?

7. Explain why the following are virtues:
   * Trust
   * Politeness
   * Tranquillity

8. Is whatever is pleasant moral? When does it become moral?

6. Kant

Immanuel Kant (1724-1804) proposed that many things of the mind have come as a part of our inheritance. Morality is one such component. We normally think that morality is something inculcated socially. How can Kant claim that it is inherited? Kant is not referring to morals of specific cultures. He says that the morality-generating code itself is inherited.

Is that code inherited in 'immoral' people too? Yes, very much, every mind is born with this code. Let us see how this code works.

Kant says every one subjects one's actions to the question: 'What if everyone / others do what I do?' He will not feel good if he thinks he is doing what others, in his opinion, should not be doing. In other words, he will feel bad if he thinks he is doing what others should not be doing. This reasoning and universalizing of his action is an inherent part in every one.

Everyone is born with this need for reasoning and universalizing to evaluate one's actions. It means the moral law is within each one of us. Kant gave a name to this need of man – *categorical imperative*. It is defined as the need "to act as if the maxim of our action were to become by our will a universal law of nature."

This categorical imperative drastically reduces man's capacity to be immoral. Not only that, it also explains how certain behavior is labeled moral or immoral: the immoral is what fails the test of categorical imperative.

How different from superego?

Freud read Kant. He was convinced that there is moral law within man and that it creates pressure on the individual to behave in socially harmless ways. He called it *superego*. *Ego* is supposed to balance the superego with the *Id*, the basic instincts of man.

But the difference is, superego is a result of conditioning. Categorical Imperative is supposed to be a result of

Kant: Categorical Imperative restricts man's capacity to be immoral.

Freud: Yes, like Superego.

reasoning. Freud conceived of conditioned superego because he tended to place heavy emphasis on the irrational forces within man.

Evaluation

1. Kant's theory is flawless. But he should have made it very clear that categorical imperative is a subjective experience. Reasoning and universalizing is done by the individual and not by others. A considerable part of the criticism of this theory was based on the critic's reasoning and universalizing, rather than the subject's.

2. An ideologically convinced terrorist will not have any sense of guilt when he reflects on his actions. He may look immoral to others. Bin Laden may have followed his categorical imperative. His superego may have been untouched by guilt.

3. A chunk of morality can be explained in terms of categorical imperative. For example, why trust is valued, or deception condemned can be explained.

4. Sexual morality can be explained in terms of the universal need for trust.

♦ ♦ ♦

Questions to think about

1. What is 'categorical imperative'?

2. How is categorical imperative different from super ego?

3. What becomes unethical as per Kant?

4. Explain why 'trustworthiness' as per Kant is a virtue.

7. Hegel

Friedrich Hegel (1770-1831) is considered a great philosopher, and Karl Marx is his most famous student. Hegel is considered to be a very abstract thinker. Though regarded as profound, his writings are known to be lacking in clarity.

His philosophy becomes clear if we first discuss certain ideas of the East that are at the core of his philosophy. There is this Eastern idea that consciousness of mankind is one. For example, J Krishnamurti believes that humans are not separated, and their consciousness is all connected. So there is something that can be called collective consciousness of mankind. Krishnamurti also believes that if the consciousness of some people undergoes a radical change, the consciousness of mankind also changes.

To Krishnamurti, individual consciousness is but a manifestation of the total consciousness. To him, realizing this is the most important thing for man. This realization is supposed to put an end to the isolation of self – which is considered the source of all conflict and sorrow.

Krishnamurti's philosophy that is advocated in the 20th

century is but a continuation of the Buddhist tradition, which Hegel uses with some modification.

Mankind is connected, Hegel accepts. That collective entity is given a name–called Spirit or Mind or the Absolute. His philosophy is introduced in *Phenomenology of Spirit* (1806) and later developed in other books including *Philosophy of Right* (1821).

Why is it called 'phenomenology'? Kant's theory that thing-in-itself can never be known and what we know is only phenomenon is assumed in Hegel's philosophy. Hence his theory is regarding the phenomenon only.

The Spirit is changing, evolving and constantly improving itself. By what processes is this Spirit changing? It is through dialectical processes. An idea (*thesis*) is believed to be true. But there are limitations to that. These limitations give rise to its opposite (*antithesis*). Soon, the contradiction between thesis and antithesis is resolved leading to *synthesis*. This is nothing but a thesis which will in future undergo a change. The dialectical process – which means resolution of contradictions – is an unending process. This is how the Spirit has been moving on.

Where is this Spirit? Is it equivalent to Christian God? No. Spirit is not external to mankind. It is not outside mankind. It is not like the Christian God that man should pray to.

How does the Spirit work? How does it improve itself? It works through humans. It employs humans. It uses the human faculties of reason and passion.

***

Hegel makes one important modification to the Buddhist tradition. Krishnamurti, for example, maintains that an individual at one go should realize that his self is a manifestation of the total. Hegel breaks this realization into stages.

Spirit works through cultures – culture is called the spirit of the people. One should align oneself with the spirit of the people, after one aligns oneself with one's own family. So to say, individualism should disappear first at the family level, and next at the society level. Since the current form of the society is nation-state, there should be no individualism at the level of nation-state. In this way, individual self should seek merger with its higher self: Spirit. Hegel also says failure of self to align itself with its larger part creates *alienation*.

Western political philosophy developed in the direction of glorifying individualism. But Hegel saw, like a Buddhist monk would, that individual self is based on ignorance and imperfect knowledge. So Hegel proposed, unlike a Buddhist monk, that individual self should align itself with that of the nation-state. The individual is for the state – in contrast to the liberals' view that the state is for the individual.

Buddha: Hegel, what you are proposing is self-aggrandizement, which is not the same as self-dissolution.

***

Where is the issue of ethics in all this? It is the individual's duty to follow the ethics of his group – his nation-state. Ethics are based on the norms of the society of which one is a part. Ethics are group ethics. They are culture-specific. To Hegel, if something is called immoral the criterion is based on what one's culture considers moral.

Are there no universal ethical principles? Hegel answers that they are not so important. They are empty and contentless. They fail to guide man in any specific way.

How about private conscience as different from what culture puts in? Can it tell us what is right or what is wrong? No, Hegel says, if individuals follow that, there will be more conflict.

Evaluation

1. Good for him that he was a poor writer. Otherwise, many would have discovered the mythology. Social sciences are better off rejecting God. Similarly, they will be better off rejecting Spirit. But it should be investigated how and in what ways human consciousness is connected.

2. Identification with bigger groups need not lead to self-realization or self-dissolution. It can be a case of self-enlargement. Selves identified with nations caused wars. This is no road to self-realization.

3. Ethics has a cultural component as well as a universal component. Not all ethics is culture-specific. For example, deception hurts one regardless of culture. Hegel misses this point.

4. It is an irony that the Buddhist idea of self-dissolution

was behind the glorification of the collective and the forced alignment of the individual self with the society at large. This ideology of forced alignment was responsible for large-scale violence in the name of Marxism.

♦♦♦

Questions to think about

1. What is 'Spirit'? How is it evolving?

2. What is phenomenology?

3. Are there no universal ethical principles? Discuss.

8. Jeremy Bentham

Jeremy Bentham (1748-1832) proposed that what is moral is what maximizes pleasure and minimizes pain. If a rule or action is found to have *utility* in promoting pleasure, then that rule or action is moral. This is the *utilitarian approach* to moral issues. Morality is a code of conduct that seeks to promote pleasure and reduce pain.

According to Bentham, pleasure should be measured in terms of its characteristics. Its 1) intensity, 2) duration, 3) certainty, 4) propinquity (how long do we have to wait for it), 5) fecundity (further pleasures that follow), 6) impurity (the pains that may ensue), and 7) effect on others should be considered in determining the morality of an action.

John Stuart Mill (1806-73) was heavily influenced by this utilitarian approach. But he felt that Bentham's scheme is only quantitative, missing on the quality of pleasure. So Mill said some are *higher pleasures* and some *lower pleasures* The higher pleasures deal with certain unique faculties of man, for example, intellectual pursuit. But who should decide whether something is a higher pleasure or a lower pleasure? Mill said experts who know the alternatives should decide that. Only those pursuing the higher pleasure know the nature and the shallowness of a lower pleasure.

To Bentham, poker and poetry are equal if they give the same amount of pleasure. Mill answered that he would rather be a discontented Socrates than a well-fed pig. Thus Mill wants to take into account both the quantity and the quality of pleasures. Mill finds that living up to certain standards, or following a code of conduct by itself, is a higher pleasure.

Utilitarianism thus considers that what is moral is what promotes the 'greatest happiness of the greatest number of persons.' It does not make any distinction between pleasure and happiness.

Evaluation A

Utilitarianism may have contributed to liberalism in politics and economics. But as a theory of ethics, it is perhaps the silliest of all. The theory may appear bold to those who equate morality with some painful religious obligation. But it is teleological for those who believe that morality has always aimed at the maximization of happiness.

Mill's introduction of a new variable of quality doesn't make any fundamental difference to Bentham's theory. It can be argued that a higher pleasure will have greater intensity, longer duration and lead to further pleasures. Thus the so called quality can be accommodated in the quantitative approach.

Evaluation B

A theory of ethics should try to answer the following

questions.

- What is that rule or action that leads to pleasure – not that whatever leads to pleasure is moral?

- What promotes pleasure in the long term though at some expense in the short term?

- How should one choose between one's pleasure and that of others? How do you distribute the given total?

Ethics is the study of such dilemmas. Utilitarianism has no answer.

Evaluation C

The theory fails to recognize the link between pleasure and pain. Can there be pleasure for one without his going through pain? Can pleasure be pursued without the possibility of pain?

Happiness is something different. It is not more pleasure and less pain. Happiness lies in rightly negotiating this pleasure-pain link, an inevitable part of our lives.

Evaluation D

The theory also misses the link between the parts and the whole. It assumes that if there is pleasure from an act, all such pleasurable acts combined give more pleasure. It is not realized that totality may work differently.

Similarly, the theory assumes that society's pleasure is the sum total of the pleasures of the individuals. But society has its own level of reality, and its complexity requires that its road to happiness be different.

So we should look for harmony, we can't simply add. Our body parts are not simply added but harmoniously integrated.

The purpose of ethics is to discover the harmony between the conflicting pleasure needs of individuals or groups.

Marx on Bentham

Karl Marx's criticism of Jeremy Bentham reveals one of the central convictions of Marx: economy shapes human nature. He wrote in Das Kapital, "The principle of utility was no discovery of Bentham. He simply reproduced in his dull way what Helvetius and other Frenchmen had said with esprit in the 18th century. To know what is useful for a dog, one must study dog-nature. This nature itself is not to be deduced from the principle of utility. The principle of utility must first deal with human nature in general, and then with human nature modified in each historical epoch. Bentham makes short work of it. With the driest naivete he takes the modern shopkeeper, especially the English shopkeeper, as the normal man. Whatever is useful to this queer normal man, and to his world, is absolutely useful. This yardstick, then, he applies to past, present and future."

So, to Marx, that "modern shopkeeper" is not a normal man! The shopkeeper's mind is so twisted he wouldn't know what might give him pleasure and what might bring him pain. He would seek to set up more shops and earn more money but may never understand the joy of sharing. The shopkeeper's calculations of what makes him happier are reflections of his twisted mind.

Marx is raising two issues here. First, man doesn't know how to maximize his pleasure. To that extent, the pleasure-maximizing theory is useless. Second, economic systems prevent man from even knowing what is pleasurable to him!

Bentham: Man should maximize pleasure and minimize pain.
Marx: But man doesn't know what gives him pleasure.
Nietzsche: Man should perish in seeking something beyond himself.

◆ ◆ ◆

Questions to think about

1. a) You are the driver of a railway trolley. While going on the main track you lose control over the brakes. You notice 5 men on the main track and one man on the side track. Would you divert the trolley to the side track?

   b) Suppose you are not the driver of the trolley, but an onlooker standing on the bridge and there is no side track. But by pushing down one fat man from the bridge, you can stop the trolley to save the lives of the five on the track. Would you do it?

2. a) You are a doctor. Five people are wounded in an accident. By ignoring one person who is severely injured, you can save the remaining four. If you do not ignore any, all five will die. What will you do?

   b) You are a doctor. Four patients require transplants of various body parts. A fifth patient requires only a minor operation. However, by taking the body parts of the fifth patient, you can save the lives of the four patients. Will you do it?

3. In 1884, in the UK, four sailors in a lifeboat got stranded. All their food was exhausted. They ate nothing for days. On the 9th day the captain said that unless one person was killed, all of them would die. So the others decided that the cabin boy, an orphan, should be killed. And he was killed. When they landed, all of them were tried. Do you think what the captain and others did was wrong?

4. In ancient Rome, Christians were thrown to lions for

the amusement of crowds. Was it right because it maximised the pleasure of the spectators though only a few were killed?

5. What do you think is the link between pleasure and pain? What is the problem with these concepts?

8   What is utility?

9. What according to Bentham is a virtue?

10. What according to Mill is a higher pleasure?

11. Do quantitative considerations affect what is moral?

12. Evaluate utilitarianism as a theory of morality.

9. Nietzsche

The philosophy of Friedrich Nietzsche (1844–1900) enables man to take a huge leap forward towards freedom. This extraordinary philosopher attempted something that no one, including religious figures, had done before.

Issues of morality, throughout history, have been discussed with a slant: how should an individual be kind towards others, how not to hurt others, how not to cheat others etc. It is understood that man by nature pursues his pleasure. But the question is, will his pursuit of pleasure obstruct that of the others? How should he be prevented from obstructing others' happiness? Still better, how should he be made to contribute to others' happiness? These have been the moral issues discussed all through the centuries.

The focus of morality has been on taming man. Enter Nietzsche. The issue is no longer how to tame man so that he may be helpful to others. The issue is how to retain, how to express, how to realize one's basic instincts. More importantly, how to express and how to pursue man's *"will to power"*?

This will to power, which Freud would later call *aggression,* is a basic instinct of man. Darwin showed – Darwinism is an important source to Nietzsche – that this instinct is the basis for the evolution of more intelligent species like man. Nietzsche noticed that Christian ethics condemn this instinct and glorify its absence. Nietzsche found that to be wrong.

In *The Genealogy of Morals* (1887) Nietzsche puts forward the idea that morality is cultural. This idea was first propounded by the sophists. Morality changes as culture changes. This idea is central to modern social sciences like Anthropology. Nietzsche attempted to trace the genealogy of morals – the ancestry of the present-day morals.

Nietzsche says Christian morality, which is of recent origin, is only one kind of morality. This morality is based on the opposition between *good* and *sin.* Nietzsche argues that what Christianity considers good and bad is inappropriate to man's progress. Christianity glorifies humility and not pride, meekness and not strength, and suffering and not success. This kind of morality doesn't encourage man to seek strength. Nietzsche calls this *slave morality.*

The ancient Greeks didn't have this slave morality. Courage, physical strength and mental strength were called *good.* Not having them was *bad.* Good corresponded to strength, bad corresponded to weakness. That, Nietzsche called *noble morality.*

Noble morality was not suddenly replaced by slave morality. It had passed through the morality that Judaism gave: glorification of ascetic values, and repudiation of physical and sensory pleasures. With Judaism began the glorification of weakness which became part of Christian ethics.

So what is wrong with Christian ethics? It represses strength. It is anti-progress. It is against human nature.

Christian morality may not make man very strong, but can't it make him at least kind towards others? Wouldn't it at least make social life easier? Nietzsche's emphatic answer: 'no'. Because Christian morality is not natural to man and society is glorifying the unnatural, man hides his real nature to look good in the eyes of others. His mind becomes twisted, corrupted, and finally unkind. What Christ values, one will not find it in man through this type of morality. So the Christian morality is both useless and dangerous.

Why then are so many trying to follow this morality? Nietzsche answers that mankind has not realized that God is dead and with Him the sin, the heaven and hell died too. Though God died due to the explosion of reason, the morality based on Him is continuing. It is time man got rid of the Christian morality the way it got rid of God.

Daringly Nietzsche thought he was offering or trying to work out the right type of morality, which is in tune with human nature, to the post-God world.

Evaluation A

Old morality didn't take into consideration Darwinism and the power of aggression in the evolution of higher species. Nietzsche's correction was very much needed. Social sciences in fact moved in the direction Nietzsche wanted – be it the theory of Realism in International Relations, or recognition of greed in Economics.

Evaluation B

Coming to Christian ethics, was Jesus wrong in insisting

on forgiveness, in glorifying pity? Do these virtues weaken individuals? Yes and no. If forgiveness/ kindness is forced either by one's own will or that of others, it leads to a twisted mind. Action that is in conflict with the mind wouldn't contribute to psychological health. On the other hand, when forgiveness/ kindness comes naturally, the mind is cleansed.

Jesus: *Now exchange blows.*

It can be argued that forgiveness is not appropriate in every case. Some should be allowed to settle disputes through punishment. What is enslaving is not pity or kindness, but the conflict between action and emotion.

Kindness/selflessness should be a result of natural flowering of the individual. Only then will it have beauty. Otherwise, the result would be twisted minds and miserable souls.

Evaluation C

There was one important incident in Nietzsche's life before he turned insane. He was standing in the balcony of his apartment upstairs when he saw on the road a horse being flogged. He ran down to save the horse and he collapsed sobbing after embracing it. From that he never recovered. It shows he was moved by kindness, an emotion against which he fought lifelong.

Kindness had probably hit him with a vengeance so hard that he never recovered to sing the praises of unkindness.

Evaluation D

Nietzsche was against the glorification of suffering. But he suffered more than Jesus. Nietzsche became insane, was sent to asylum and brought home only to lead a meaningless life on bed for a decade. Why did he suffer when he didn't value suffering?

In fact suffering is only in the eyes of the people who do not know the true source of happiness. Socrates did not suffer taking poison; Jesus didn't suffer on the cross; nor did Nietzsche suffer doing things that turned him insane. They would willingly do what they did again and again.

Nietzsche did what Jesus had done long ago— but declaring himself anti-Christ. For people to notice and understand the importance of what he was teaching, Christ too might call himself anti-Christ if born again.

♦ ♦ ♦

Questions to think about

1. Do you agree with Nietzsche that
   a) aggression is biological?
   b) will to power is desirable?
   c) kindness is undesirable?
   d) equality is a wrong value?
   e) gender equality is nonsense?
   f) democracy is a wrong ideal?
   g) morals evolve over a period of time?

2. Do you consider Nietzsche's teachings an obstacle in creating a better society?

3. Is an interpretation of Darwinism different from Nietzsche's possible?

10. Thomas Hobbes

Historically, many religious prophets and philosophers have glorified how man's intrinsic nature has been good and that it can be better. Rarely has it been proposed that man's basic nature, as he is born with, may be anti-social. So if a social scientist writes a big book on the assumption that man's basic nature is anti-social, it is bound to be a provocative one. That was exactly what Thomas Hobbes (1588-1679) did through his book *Leviathan* (1651). Hobbes's arguments continue to be provocative because moral teaching, inculcated among the social scientists as well as lay people, continues to be what it used to be.

It is not that most people believe that man is basically good and that Hobbes shocked them by saying that he is not. Most people believe that man may not be basically good but it is not a matter of conviction with them. Hobbes has a conviction on the matter.

Historians regard Hobbes or Machiavelli as the forerunners of modern political thought. Both are known for negative assumptions. These negative assumptions are the result of fresh thinking, unhindered by moralism. In a way, the modern period started with the discovery of evil in man.

This discovery in the case of Hobbes is the direct result of the scientific revolution. Hobbes dwelt at length on methods of science as it progressed till Galileo. 'Scientific method' meant theorizing on the basis of what *is* rather than what should be. It meant courage to question the age-old assumptions. Hobbes thought he was doing just that – exposing stark human nature.

State of nature is "a war of everyone against everyone[1]," wrote Hobbes. "I put for the general inclination of all mankind, a perpetual and restless desire of power after power that ceases only in death." Why is he not contented with some power? "Because he can't assure the power and means to live well, which he has at present, without the acquisition of more[2]."

State of nature is a state of war, which no one benefits from. People are full of desire and fear. So they enter into a contract with one another to transfer their power to a sovereign. Monarchy, Hobbes argued, is an outcome of such a contract. People did not have direct contract with the king, but they surrendered their power to the king as a result of contract among themselves.

Did Hobbes mean that people assembled at one time and actually did this? No. The historical sequence is not important but what is important is what role the sovereign is performing now and what would happen if he did not perform that role. State of nature is a thought experiment. The experiment reveals that law is in everyone's interest and that law can be implemented only with a centralized power.

---

1. I discussed this statement in detail in *Sociological Thought*
2. All quotations from *Western Political Thought* by Brian R. Nelson

Leviathan (means something extremely large and powerful) is thus inevitably generated out of the need for order, given human nature. The cover page of *Leviathan* depicts supreme power that is made of individuals holding military power in one hand and church power in the other.

Hobbes's defence of monarchy when people were fighting against it was, in a way, a regressive idea. Yet in another way it was an advanced idea because kings then claimed divine right to rule. Hobbes was positing that kings had no such right and their legitimacy was based on social contract. And with some refinement, Locke was to develop a version in tune with the democratic aspirations of the people.

Relevance to IR theory

Freud's super ego and Kant's categorical imperative are no doubt appropriate correctives. In IR theory, Hobbes remains an influential figure. *Realists* consider the state of nature assumption as valid when it comes to relationship between states. Unlike the individuals within a state who are ruled by a central power, states are not controlled by one power. So they fear and seek power, more and more of it.

◆ ◆ ◆

Questions to think about

1. What according to Hobbes is the state of nature?

2. What do you know about the social contract theory?

3. How is Hobbes's theory an advance over the divine right theory?

4. Who is the main source of inspiration to Hobbes?

5. What do you know about the Realist theory?

11. John Locke

We are all very familiar with the ideas of the English philosopher John Locke (1632-1704) because it is by his ideas that modern political institutions are governed. Locke, like Hobbes, believed in the social contract theory of government. But Locke made such modifications to the contract theory of Hobbes that are up-to-date with the democratic aspirations of the English people. Locke presented his political ideas in two books: *First* and *Second Treatise of Government.*

Hobbes derived his contract theory from the assumptions made on state of nature. The negativity in man made the sovereign essential. Locke was not intimidated by Hobbes's assumptions of state of nature. Man is not such an evil as Hobbes depicted. Nor was man so good that he would not require to contract out power to one centre.

So Locke thought man was not so power-hungry as Hobbes depicted – man required to hand over power for the creation of a better and orderly society. Thus Locke's state-of-nature assumptions are not provocative – either negatively or positively.

Locke retains the contractual nature of the government without portraying man as an evil.

What is the nature of contract between the people and the government? The contract is not to hand over absolute power to the centre. Hobbes's theory gives absolute power to the centre, Locke's only limited power. Handing over absolute power to the monarch as Hobbes argued is inconsistent with Hobbes's own assumptions of man. "Absolute monarchs are but men[1]," unless checked, they would abuse power.

Under Locke's scheme, people would give only limited power to the government. Individuals will have certain rights that can never be taken away by the state. Right to life and right to religious belief are examples. How is the abuse of even the limited power checked? If there is abuse the government should be replaced. It means there should be a periodic assessment of the performance of the government. By what processes should this assessment take place? For that there should be a legislature periodically elected and it should judge whether the government is properly using the power given to it by the people.

The function of the legislature is not only to elect or remove the government but also pass the laws by which the government should conduct its business. Should all legislators agree on a law for it to be passed? Not necessary. Majority opinion would do, unanimity is not required. In giving these roles to the legislature, Locke is actually proposing distribution of power. This distribution is supposed to be a check against the abuse of power.

That Locke is proposing institutional arrangements to check abuse of power implies that if unchecked, man abuses power.

---

1. All quotations are from *Western Political Thought* by Brian R. Nelson

So in a way, Locke is not moving far from Hobbes's assumption of what man truly is.

Right to property

Locke is considered to be the father of liberal democracy. Liberalism means two things: individualism and belief in a limited state. Belief in the rights of individuals constitutes the core of liberalism. But what are these rights that no government can take away?

One such right, Locke believed, is the right to property. To him right to life means right to one's own labour and the fruits of that labour, which is property. "The labour of his body and the work of his hands.. are properly his."

Will one's right to property clash with that of others? Not always. "Whatsoever then he removes out of the state that nature has provided, and left it in, he has mixed his labour with, and joined to it something that is his own, and thereby makes it his property. It being by him removed from the common state nature has placed it in, it has by this labour something annexed to it, that excludes the common right of other men."

So it becomes yours if you add something to what is in state of nature. What if others also want to add their labour and own what was previously common? Locke adds a condition to acquiring property by saying "at least where there is enough, and as good left in common for others."

So theoretically, you can't take something scarce, add labour to own it and exclude others. But even theoretically, there are no limits placed on how much property one can own or the minimum labour one has to put in to claim as one's own what one did not previously own.

Would not accumulation by some lead to inequalities? Of course they would and that is justifiable. "God gave the world to men in common; but it can't be supposed He meant it should always remain common and uncultivated. He gave it for the use of the industrious and rational, not to the fancy or covetousness of the quarrelsome and contentious."

That was a very provocative statement – but essence of capitalism. That essence is being declared in the name of a protestant ethic, in the name of God, in the name of Jesus, who, all evidence shows, regarded the rich as 'the fancy' and not the other way round.

The history of the 20th century was in a way a debate on this right to property. Disagreeing with this right to property, some chose to create systems that disagreed with liberalism itself, rather democracy itself.

◆ ◆ ◆

◆ ◆ ◆

Questions to think about

1. What according to Locke is the state of nature?

2. What modifications did Locke make to Hobbes's theory?

3. What is the importance of fundamental rights to Locke?

4. How did Locke defend the Right to Property?

12. Rousseau

Jean-Jacques Rousseau (1712-78) is a hugely influential thinker, who impacted modern political thought and the institutions. To the extent he impacted the world, he can be held responsible for the errors of mankind. Rousseau, in my opinion, is one thinker who misled the world, for which the world paid a very heavy price. It is unfortunate that flaws in Rousseau did not become part of common knowledge that political science imparts.

While other Enlightenment thinkers were glorifying reason and were sure of human progress, Rousseau took a critical stand on the issue. It has the following implications:

- Taking a counter stand, if it is challenging enough, in itself contributes to critical reflection on the mainstream view. In that sense, Rousseau did make a positive contribution to Enlightenment. He used reason to criticize reason, his supporters as well as his critics used reason to defend or criticize reason – reinforcing the tradition of Enlightenment.

- Taking a stand counter to the mainstream current is in itself a source of inspiration to the rebels of all ages – Marx, Gandhi, who were influenced thus, were no exception.

But the tragedy is, if there is a serious flaw in the theory and rebels take it up seriously and go about impacting the world, people will end up paying a heavy price for it. The 20th century carried the burden of Rousseau.

Rousseau said man was using reason for self-interest. He was using knowledge to show his superiority over others. All that was self-interest rather than promotion of goodness of society. There is no flaw in that argument. Hobbes said it before. Freud was to say it later.

The flaw is that Rousseau attributed this tendency of man to pursue self-interest, which can be at the expense of others, to inequalities in the society. He did it in a systematic, comprehensive way. That no one had done before.

Man's pursuit of power, using reason for this, is no way of progressing. What is important is not promotion of reason, but kindness. What is important is welfare of the society, not hankering after power over fellow beings. How can this be accomplished?

There need not be absolute equality among the people, but inequalities should not be such that one can have power over others. Property can't be a matter of right, unlimited accumulation of property is of course bad for the society. Locke is wrong. Over such a near-egalitarian society, appropriate political institutions should be created.

What are those institutions? All people should have the right to vote in a legislature. They do not send their representatives.

All together should decide what is good for them. Because they are equal, what is good for one is good for all. Private interest and public interest will match. Utility, which is based on self-interest, then coincides with virtue, which is the basis of good for others.

What such an assembly wills, Rousseau called *general will.* Following general will is in the interest of all. That general will is moral. It is the source of liberty. What if some individuals do not see it that way and disagree with the general will? Well, they are wrong. If they do not recognize it, they do not see the beauty of the arrangement. They do not understand how or why their perception is wrong. They should be educated to understand that the general will enhances their freedom. Rousseau declared famously, they should be "forced to be free!"

We know now that mass murders were committed in forcing people to freedom – from the French Revolution to Stalin.

Notice too the idea that man does not know his own means of freedom. What makes him free should be forcibly inculcated in him. This idea Marx picked up later and said only communism would end alienation, and if man does not realize this, it is his ignorance!

Twentieth century history proved Locke was right and Rousseau wrong. It is important to respect individual rights, create political institutions that enhance individual freedom. How about inequalities? Try to see that some basic rights are not accessible to power or hierarchy, which is what Locke stood for.

Theoretically, what is the flaw in Rousseau? It is in thinking that inequalities gave rise to self-interest and power. The truth is the other way round. It is self-interest and aggression that led to inequalities under certain appropriate technological conditions, which Marx called surplus. Aggression is far more ancient than inequalities which are a product of certain stage in culture. Aggression can't end with the abolition of inequalities. It is a part of biology, and not of culture.

On the practicality of the general will taking care of everyone, in addition to equality, Rousseau said state should be small and only then would direct democracy be possible. But the theory is wrong regardless of the size. The theory is wrong even at a village level, why even at family level! Imagine every family member going by what the family by consensus or by majority arrives at!

Man surrenders his freedom to a monarch in Hobbes's theory and to a crowd in Rousseau's theory. Only in Locke's theory is individuality preserved.

♦ ♦ ♦

Rousseau : *The majority knows how to free you. If you do not agree with it, you will be forced to be free.*

Questions to think about

1. What does Rousseau mean by 'general will'?

2. Should people be forced to follow the 'general will'?

3. Are selfishness and desire for power outcomes of inequalities?

4. Do inequalities wreck the working of democracy?

13. Edmund Burke

The violence of the French Revolution made many people wonder what went wrong with the Revolution. One man, Edmund Burke (1729-97), seemed to have provided the answer. His theory seemed very authentic because he gave the reasons not after the terror but before it. While his contemporaries thought that the French Revolution was only a continuation of the English and the American, Burke had the insight to see the difference and predict disastrous consequences. Because of the generality of the things he said, his *Reflections on the Revolution in France* (1790) gave rise to a school of political thought called conservatism, as opposed to liberalism.

Though his political philosophy came to be known as conservatism, Burke was not the one who would blindly defend the existing social or political arrangement. Burke had argued in favour of the American Revolution. He had supported the ideals of the Glorious Revolution. So he had not been a defender of the status quo. It was just that he found that the ideology of the French Revolution was unique in certain ways and that ideology was bound to bring terrible consequences to the society.

The English and American revolutions attempted to change certain political arrangements at the top. They did not try to reorder the society, which the French Revolution was attempting. If the change at the top was good, would not its extension to the bottom be good as well?

Burke does not think so. Change beyond a certain point leads not just to repairing the bad but can even damage what is good. Why is this so? Because society is integrated, if you destroy an institution the consequences of it will be felt widely, and they can be bad. During the French Revolution, in the name of equality aristocracy was destroyed, and in the name of reason religious order was destroyed.

Burke said if we destroy the old institutions, we take away the processes by which power is decentralised and man is protected from the abuse of power. He said chaos resulting from destruction of the old systems of authority forces people to prefer a dictator, "the master of your assembly, the master of your whole republic[1]." This the French did in Napoleon.

If the ideology of the French Revolution is wrong, does it mean that Rousseau is wrong? Does it mean Locke is wrong? Burke's answer is 'yes'. To Burke, they are wrong not simply in specifics but in a fundamental way. Both propose that in a state of nature, man was born with certain rights and man, for his own good, chose to give up some of the rights to the society. To Burke, this idea of forgoing rights to society is not only ahistorical but also logically false, for man has never existed and will never exist outside his society. Man is not away from his society. "The state of civil society is a state of nature," proclaims Burke.

---

1. All the quotations are from Brian R. Nelson

"Man is born free, yet everywhere he is in chains," wrote Rousseau. It unleashed mobs to demand their lost rights. But to Burke, man is not born free anywhere and is somewhat free everywhere.

Leaving the historical context aside, what does Burke have to say about how to change society? He wants to retain some and change others but never destroy wholesale. "A disposition to preserve, and an ability to improve, taken together, would be my standard of a statesman." Surely that is something all rebels should ponder over.

Evaluation

In modern terminology, we know a part of computer can be formatted only from another part. One needs to stand on something to change other things. French revolutionaries stood on nothing. That is why the French Revolution was a disaster.

♦ ♦ ♦

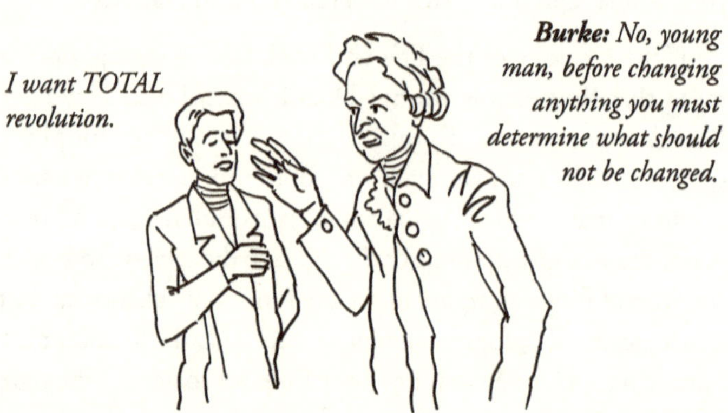

Questions to think about

1. What is Burke's explanation of the French Revolution?

2. What according to Burke is the state of nature? How is it different from other states?

3. What is the right way of changing a society?

14. John Rawls

John Rawls (1921-2002) provided an extremely simple as well as very creative way of looking at the issue of justice that received much attention from ancient times. Many before Rawls discussed why something was just, why something was not just, what contributes to the wellbeing of the society, and what does not.

Through his *A Theory of Justice* (1971) and its revisions, Rawls does not say this particular allocation or that particular behavior is just. Instead he suggests a way by which what is just can be discovered by the people themselves – on any issue. And the people, he says, wouldn't even disagree on what is just – if his method was followed! What is just is not what is well articulated by a philosopher, or what is believed to be just by the majority but that which is unanimously felt to be so!

All think alike. All agree on what is justice. That is what Rawls said. Why then are people everywhere debating among themselves claiming that only their position is just? Should women be given reservations in jobs? Should Muslims be given reservations? Should we apply the creamy layer concept in the reservations to dalits? Should we encourage inter-caste marriages? On any of these questions, people take positions and argue this side or that side. So how can Rawls say that all will agree on what is justice and that all think alike?

To Rawls, and to many thinkers before him, if people are arguing in a particular way, it is because their material position influences their viewpoint. Women want reservations, men oppose. Muslims want reservations, Hindus oppose. Similarly other issues. People argue in a particular way that their viewpoint enhances their material position.

And Rawls says all will think alike if only they do not know what their position is going to be in the society they are going to be a part of. What they think just when they do not know what their position is going to be is what is just. It is as simple as that.

So the principles people agree to when they don't know their positions are the principles of justice, by which a society should be guided. Rawls calls this condition of not knowing their positions in advance *veil of ignorance*. People do not know their class, social position, gender, religion, and abilities – physical or psychological.

Rawls also makes certain assumptions that are reasonable:

● People value certain things: rights, liberties, powers, opportunities, income, wealth, bases of self-respect. These are called primary goods. Notice that these goods include material as well as non-material ones. So comprehensive are these goods that choosing their distribution means choosing social, economic and political structure of the society.

- People want to maximize these primary goods. (Unlike the monks who want to minimize them!)

- Society has a moderate scarcity of the goods. Resources enough but not so much that there is no scope for conflict.

- They are not gamblers. They don't choose a principle, gambling on a particular position for themselves.

- They are not envious of others. Nor are they altruistic, desiring others' welfare at the expense of their own. (Unlike some religious people who believe in certain ideologies glorifying charity! Interestingly, Rawls says people don't have any prior conception of what is good!)

- They can't leave the society after their position is known. They can enter at birth, exit only at death.

This set of assumptions along with the veil of ignorance is called *original position*. What people choose in the original position is what is just.

But what is it that they will choose? Or rather, what are the principles they will choose by which the goods are to be distributed?

Three principles

(1) There should be equal liberty where each person is guaranteed a set of basic liberties. These include the rights to free speech, association, conscience, thought, property, a fair trial, vote, hold political office.

(2a) There must be equal access to jobs and services under fair equality of opportunity.

(2b) Inequalities are only justified if they benefit the least advantaged members of the society. This is called *difference principle*.

But these principles are conflicting. So Rawls gives their order of priority: (1) > (2a) > (2b)

Freedom to have a family should be granted even if it violates equality of opportunity. That is to say (1) should take precedence over (2a), the principle of equal opportunity.

Why would people choose (2b), the difference principle?

Rawls thinks that people will choose, of all possible distribution arrangements, *maximin,* which maximizes the goods to those with minimum advantages. They will not choose *maximax,* which maximizes goods to those with maximum advantages. Nor will they choose absolute equality – they don't want to rule out for themselves the possibility of having more. Instead, they will choose maximin out of concern that they may belong to the least advantaged group. The marginal utility of a thing at lower levels is much higher than at higher levels. So maximax would be preferred to maximin. And the difference principle realizes maximin.

These principles as well as their order of importance is what people will choose in the original position. So following them should create a just society.

♦ ♦ ♦

Marx: *A just society is one where everyone contributes as per one's capacity and takes only as per one's need.*

Rawls: *That would make a very unjust society.*

Questions to think about

1. What is meant by veil of ignorance?

2. What are primary goods?

3. What is meant by original position?

4. What is the difference principle?

5. What are the principles that are followed in a just society?

15. On gods

Before discussing Moses, Jesus or Muhammad I would like to make a few observations about God or gods. Those three prophets claimed close relationship with God. How can a man in the 21st century understand such claims?

On matters of religion, I proceed with certain assumptions – obvious to me, but need not be so to others. One of the things that I assume – without the slightest desire to debate – is that there is no God. Who then created the world? Someone, most probably god's nephew who died soon afterwards!

Anyway, even if God created the world, how can we know that He whom we are worshipping is the same one who created it? How can we also assume that the same God is still engaged in running life and granting favors to his devotees?

Too obvious for me is that man created gods as well as devils. Man's world of desires and fears extends beyond what is known and the world of gods and devils is created. This to me is self-evident.

So if someone says, 'God spoke to me', what do we make of it? It does not mean he is uttering a lie. He is only referring to his deeply felt inner voice.

Will that be truth? Possibly, but only to the extent his knowledge and intellect permit. And it will never be independent of the circumstances he is in. After all it is the truth of a man.

How does one explain 'spiritual experiences' involving physiological changes? Deeper psychological processes cause some corresponding physiological changes. One need not posit an external agent to explain these changes.

How about miracles – parting of oceans, healing of leprosy patients by touch? They are interesting stories made up to prove how God is on the side of the messenger.

While dismissing gods, we are as well dismissing claims of someone being a 'son of God', or a 'messenger of God'. To us, a 'revelation' is no more than a man's high-end truth.

With those assumptions we can read the past, and try to separate the myth from the possible reality. We will never know what really happened. But by eliminating the supernatural elements, we can get closer to the real.

We should ask: how did they become prophets, what are their values, why did they preach what they preached, and what is the context of their message? This is the way we need to explore any religion. The way we read Socrates should be the way we read Jesus – with curiosity, with respect and with an attitude of learning.

We should try to see in their teaching what is valid for all times and what is only time-specific, that is, valid only for their time. I think the idea of messenger of God is itself time-specific. In Homer's Odyssey, written in the 8th century BC, we see that gods then were very close to people! Using modern jargon, we can say there was a class of gods existing just above the class of humans. Gods were guiding humans, rewarding them and punishing them. There was a close rapport between gods and humans with so many intermediaries, such as oracles, priests, facilitating inter-class communication!

Men taking messages from gods was not rare in the ancient world. Women conceiving through gods was also not an unusual thing. Alexander's mother thought she had conceived him through Zeus, the king of gods. Alexander himself wondered if his mother was right.

Man's proximity to gods explains why prophets explained certain important things in terms of gods. Prophets didn't invent gods. They didn't cheat people. They didn't lie. The ancient societies happened to be living closer to gods.

And what is true of the ancient world is true of many simple societies. Islam though it emerged in the 7th century AD came from such simple societies.

***

Why can't the world take Jesus just the way it takes Socrates?

Religion, when founded by a man – not all are founded, for example, Hinduism – first begins with some rebellious thought system. Some people are influenced by the thought system. They become its adherents. But unlike other thought systems, this particular thought system is associated with some supernatural elements, which the adherents don't question. Soon the adherents lose track of why they chose the thought system and convert the thought system into their identity. We can then say a religion is born.

Conversion of a thought system to a group identity is at the centre of division of mankind into many religious groups. Thus we have Buddhists, Christians, Muslims, and Sikhs.

When a thought system becomes a group identity, learning stops. Dogma replaces doubt. Intolerance sets in. The adherents become capable of doing just the opposite of what the founder may have said or meant!

Will some thought systems lose more than others when they become identities? It appears so. When a thought system is generated in a primitive society it becomes more irrelevant when people of advanced societies want to blindly follow it. Islam is a case in point. When a thought system contains too many specific details then also it loses more of its spirit or the original intent. Islam again is one such example.

***

Some prophets insisted that there is only one God. And they were uncompromising in their belief that there is only one God. Let us see why it was imperative for them to insist on one God.

Values and morals in those days were stated in supernatural terms, and their violation was supposed to invite supernatural wrath. Morals got closely linked with the gods. To say that there is only one God is to posit that there is only moral system. This is to emphasize that contrary morals are wrong. This is similar to a modern nation having only one constitution, insisting that no law should violate that.

***

When man created God, he created Him in terms of his ideals – according to his ideas of the nature of reality and notions of truth. Man struggles to know the truth that is relevant and valid for all times. Man wants to somehow arrive at such a truth. What man wants to possess he thinks God already possesses. He thinks God knows the truth which is valid for all times. He can't think that God may be using the trial-and-error method like him to arrive at truth.

Man thinks that if God said something it should be ultimate and unalterable truth. God can't contradict Himself. God can't say 'I thought like that then, but now I think differently'.

A story in Islam goes that Prophet Muhammad once received a revelation asking him to accept other gods of Mecca and later another revelation that the earlier revelation was wrong and that it had actually been sent by Satan. This leads the unbelievers to think that many other revelations may have been inspired by Satan whereas the believers argue that this story itself is wrong. This controversy regarding the Satanic verses reflects that both believers and unbelievers assume that God can't contradict Himself. They find it hard to accept that God enjoys learning!

***

One of the most serious challenges in understanding a religion is unravelling the link between the life of the messenger and his message. Those believing in revealed religion think that message is revealed and the messenger led a perfect life. If one doesn't believe in God and hence in the messages from Him, how should one approach this issue?

I believe a messenger learns from life. Learning, by its very nature, involves deviation from the prescribed. The messenger would approve of some deviations and reject some others. What he approves of becomes part of his teaching.

So the point is that it is wrong to look in the life of a messenger for perfect behavior all the time. It is also wrong to judge him on the basis of whether he has always followed what he preached. For it is from following and not following that he arrives at his message.

It is my conviction that a messenger lives in a sin-free world, in the sense that the notions of sin are inapplicable to him — for he is trying to find out, in the first place, what is sinful and what is not.

But by what criterion should the life of a messenger be judged? Only one criterion: the honesty of his search for truth. He should investigate life and report the findings to the people of his age.

***

Questions to think about

1. Do you believe in God and in His messengers?

2. Do you believe in miracles? Explain your answer.

3. When can you say a religion is born?

4. What is the link between religion and morality?

5. By what criterion should a messenger be judged?

6. How is religion defined? What is meant by world religions?

7. Why does a religion play a divisive role?

8. Why is truth converted into identity?

9. Should one be a true Hindu/ true Muslim or should one critically reflect on one's own religion?

16. Muhammad

Mecca was the place where Muhammad was born in 571 AD. Well-water there supported a small community. Otherwise, the people of the region were nomads. The importance of Mecca grew when a new caravan trade route to Syria developed from Yemen via Mecca because wars disrupted travel through Iraq. Trade brought the Meccans in contact with the cultures of new people.

Even before Muhammad, Mecca was known to be not only a trade center but also a religious center. There was a cubical shrine called Ka'ba which contained a black stone that was believed to have divine attributes. There were hundreds of gods in and around the Ka'ba, but with Allah as a high god. Arabian tribes across the region used to visit Mecca to worship these gods.

The societies around were so primitive that tribal feuds were common. If a member of a clan murdered a member of another clan, the entire clan of the murderer was held responsible for the murder. Such a pursuit of revenge – life for life – can sometimes lead to endless blood feuds.

These people did not come under any state; so there was no judiciary where the accused could be asked to defend his action before being punished.

However, the place around the Ka'ba was considered sacred and acknowledged by common consent to be revenge-free. Also tribes were supposed not to resort to violence in certain months during which Mecca turned into a market-place.

These details are important for they tell us about the culture in which Muhammad was born. He was not born in an advanced empire – like Jesus, who was born in the Roman

Empire. Nor was he born in a culture that had gone through centuries of philosophical speculation – like the Buddha who was born after the Vedas and some Upanishads.

Muhammad belonged to Quraysh, the leading tribe of Mecca. This tribe maintained the Ka'ba and monetarily benefited from it. But Muhammad was born in a poor family. His father, Abd-Allah, died even before Muhammad was born and his mother, Amina, died when he was only six years. He was looked after for two years by his grandfather after whose death Muhammad came under the protection of his uncle, Abu-Talib.

Muhammad did not receive any formal education. He was illiterate. Accompanying his uncle to distant places like Syria for the purpose of trade, Muhammad received his learning from fellow travelers and from new places, new customs and new ideas.

To his uncle, Muhammad was just an orphan. His uncle refused to give Muhammad his daughter in marriage. But a rich widow, Khadija, who was impressed by Muhammad's handling of her business, chose to marry Muhammad. Khadija was then 40 years and Muhammad was 15 years younger to her.

Soon Muhammad became a successful businessman. He had wealth, an admiring wife and children through her. Settled and successful, he should have been a happy man.

But he was not. Like many religious seekers before him, he was confronted by bigger issues of life. With his wife and children he used to go to Mount Hira for relaxation. Later he started going alone and staying in a cave for hours reflecting on life.

On one such occasion, in 610, Muhammad underwent a great spiritual experience. It was frightening at first: he felt life was being squeezed out of him.

A voice said, 'recite' (It said 'iqra' which means read or recite.)

Muhammad said, 'I can't', as he was illiterate.

Again, the voice said, 'recite.'

He said 'I can't. I don't know how.'

The voice said yet again, 'recite.'

Then he said, 'What shall I recite?'

 The voice then said,

'Recite, in the name of the Lord who created – created man from a blood-clot.

Recite, for the Lord is bountiful, who taught by the pen, taught man what he knew not.'

Muhammad at first didn't know what to make of this experience. Khadija, after consulting her kinsman Waraqa, told him that God talked to Muhammad the same way God had talked to Moses centuries ago.

That first recitation became the first poem of Qur'an (the recitation). Khadija is considered the first Muslim for she was the first one to believe that it was the message of God.

***

In today's world Islam is regarded as one of the major religions along with others like Judaism and Christianity. It is being debated what Muslims' attitude should be towards other religions and whether Muhammad respected other religions.

The context of the evolution of Islam sheds light on such questions. Islam is one of the latest religions. Christianity had emerged seven centuries before Islam; Judaism much before Christianity. The society of Muhammad was very primitive, and the context of Muhammad makes it clear that Muhammad was only trying to give to his people what advanced societies had already got.

Muhammad was comparing the primitive religion of the Arabs and trying to bring to his people the elements of advanced religions like Judaism and Christianity. He regarded himself not a challenger to Moses or Jesus but their equal – as another messenger of God.

What do we mean by an advanced religion? Are there advanced gods also? Yes, very much. Take local village goddesses in India who are not a part of the Hindu tradition. Some prayers and rituals are associated with them. But they do not have any elaborate ethical or moral code associated with them. Primitive gods and religions are like that. Advanced gods have higher philosophies and more inclusive moral codes. World religions are like that.

Muhammad proposed a higher moral code. Probably there had been nothing like kindness towards a person outside a clan. Muhammad talked about being kind towards the poor and held it as man's responsibility towards others regardless of their clans.

What a commonplace idea is to a member of an advanced religion is revolutionary to a member of a primitive religion. For example, the idea that God is merciful originated from an advanced religion. Primitive religions have brutish gods who may take revenge on people for the silliest of reasons.

The Day of Judgment – where one is judged after death on how well he lived and thereby disposed to heaven or hell – is again a concept of advanced religions. Anthropologists tell us that the concept of heaven and hell did not exist before the emergence of stratification.

Muhammad started preaching among his close people first. He formulated one of the central tenets of Islam 'There is no god, but Allah'.

How does one get to know what Allah expects from his people? There Muhammad said that he alone was the messenger. And what is the message? That consists of a series of revelations that occurred to Muhammad, which are finally codified in the Qur'an.

What if people refuse to believe this? What if they violate Allah's code? What if they don't live up to what Allah decrees? They will be judged after their death, and the sentence will be awarded then.

One God, that is Allah; One messenger, that is Muhammad; Hell, if He is not followed. This is what Muhammad taught. To this, one should submit. This is *Islam*, which means submission.

But why should people listen to him? Why did others trust him at all? The reason was his message – its power, its relevance. His followers in Mecca used to secretly assemble to listen to him. It was a moral code far superior to what they were familiar with. A code if followed would lead to better societies, better relationships. It was a new way of living and thinking.

Muhammad was no different in this from the previous prophets. Moses and Jesus won their followers through the power of their messages. Muhammad was only doing what the previous prophets had done.

Are we saying that Muhammad borrowed from others just the way we borrow ideas of science from advanced countries? No. Muhammad didn't see himself as the one spreading the ideas of other prophets. He saw himself as equal to them. He didn't see himself as either superior to them or inferior to them. He saw himself as being in the long line of messengers. He respected other messengers as much as he respected himself. His point was that he was equal to others.

When Muhammad asserted that he alone was the messenger he meant that only he was the messenger for the people he was talking to. It was not to say that Jesus was not a messenger. When he affirmed that 'there is no god, but Allah', he was rejecting only the pagan gods of Mecca. He was not rejecting the God that Jesus had referred to. In Muhammad's opinion, Moses and Jesus and many others – 1,24,000, it is said – were sent only by Allah. Allah is God for all, not just to the followers of Muhammad. When Muhammad criticized the non-believers he did not mean Christians or Jews, who were called '*People of the Book*' for they had already got revealed scriptures.

Do we know how Jerusalem became important to Muslims? According to the Islamic tradition, in what would be known as *Night Journey* Muhammad was taken by Angel Gabriel from Mecca to Dome of Rock in Jerusalem in a few seconds where he met some prophets – including Abraham, Moses and Jesus. After meeting them, Muhammad ascended to heaven where he came very close to Allah. It was during this time that Muhammad was instructed to tell his followers to pray five times a day. 'Salat' (the prayer) involved kneeling on the ground and touching it with the forehead in acknowledgement of man's smallness before God. For many years, Muslims prayed in the direction of Jerusalem.

This Dome of Rock, now also called Golden Mosque, is the place towards which Jews turn during the prayer. Jerusalem became the third holiest place for Muslims after Mecca and Medina. This reflects the importance Muhammad gave to the early religions and the messengers before him.

***

Muhammad's criticism of the gods of the Ka'ba brought him into direct confrontation with the Quraysh. Meccan authorities were hurt that the gods of the Ka'ba had been made irrelevant. If Muhammad was accepted, there would be no pilgrims and no income from running the Ka'ba. First they tried to convince Muhammad through his uncle and guardian Abu-Talib, who was also the chief of the Hashim clan. But Muhammad was not convinced. They then resorted to violence against those followers, like slaves, who did not have clan protection.

Sensing this, Muhammad thought it best to send some Muslims to Abyssinia (which is in the present-day Ethiopia) which was then ruled by a kind Christian king, Negus. Meccan authorities tried to convince the king to send back the Muslims. But the king did not oblige. It is said the king was moved by a reference to Jesus that Muslims quoted from Muhammad's teachings.

The Meccan authorities also decided on boycott of the Muslims. Non-Muslims were forbidden to sell anything to Muslims or buy anything from them. Social interactions were banned. But within two years of this boycott, there was resistance from non-Muslims. The boycott had therefore to be lifted.

Meanwhile Muhammad's reputation as a preacher was spreading outside Mecca. Some pilgrims from Yathrib (later known as Medina, meaning the city of the Prophet) met Muhammad and were impressed by him. As more and more people from Medina took an interest in Muhammad's teachings, they finally invited him to settle in Medina.

What made people from Medina want to know about Allah? Why did they want to listen to Muhammad and his prophecies on the Day of Judgment? Was it that they were afraid of going to hell otherwise?

It was not that. Tribes at Medina were quarreling among themselves. They fought a big battle of Bu'ath in 618. When people from Medina heard about Muhammad, the message was very different. It proposed new ideas, formulated new ideals, talked about one God. And they knew Muhammad was a man of honesty and integrity – a man to be trusted and respected. The people there felt – not all of them but some – Muhammad could settle their disputes forever and bring peace to the town.

After Abu-Talib died in 619 – Khadija too died the same year – leadership of the clan passed on to a fierce critic of Muhammad, Abu-Lahab. The life of the Muslims was becoming miserable. Muhammad decided to send his followers in small groups to Medina secretly, without his opponents noticing it.

Muhammad, Abu-Bakr (who was close to Muhammad and only two years younger to him) and Ali (Abu-Talib's son, then a boy of 9 or 10 years) were the last to leave. When Meccan leaders got to know of this emigration, they wanted to kill Muhammad.

To avoid blood feud with Muhammad's clan, they thought of taking one strong man from each clan and simultaneously stab Muhammad so that Muhammad's clan wouldn't know the clan of the assassin. But in the event, Muhammad got to know of this plot and escaped unhurt. This migration of Muslims to Medina, which took place in 622, is called Hijra (Emigration). The Islamic calendar begins with this year, unlike the Christian that begins with the birth of Jesus.

*****

Jesus knew that his own disciples would deny any knowledge of him. He knew one of the disciples would sell him to the Romans for a few pieces of silver. But he chose just to witness their ignorance. He was prepared to forgive them.

Muhammad's approach was completely different. If he only wanted to witness the violence that could be done to him without fighting back, all his followers would have been wiped out. His society was primitive and brutal.

Of such a society of quarreling tribes, Muhammad tried to create a state as much civilized as possible. At Medina, he tried that. The people there were mostly pagans along with some Jews. Muhammad undertook the task of arriving at a common set of principles that would make peaceful living across various tribes and faiths possible. That set of principles is also called 'constitution of Medina'. This constitutes rules against the practice of private justice based on vengeance.

The constitution did not aim to convert others to Islam. Non-Muslims were allowed to practice their own faith. Plurality was respected. In fact *Ummah*, meaning community, included non-Muslims as well. The mosque then was a place meant not only for worship by Muslims but also for all the community activities of Muslims as well as non-Muslims. Muhammad lived around. He was the guide and the judge not only for his followers but for others as well.

96

In modern times, a nation is not supposed to invade another nation. But in ancient and medieval times, a state, if it was powerful enough, could invade another state. In Muhammad's Arabia, raids on caravans to raise money were common.

In 624, Muhammad planned one such raid on a Meccan caravan coming from Syria. The Meccans got to know of his plan, changed the route of the caravan and sent an army of 1000 men to intercept Muhammad's army at Badr. Though the Meccan army was almost 3 times larger than Muhammad's, it was defeated. This was Muhammad's first battle in the name of God and the victory enhanced his prestige.

The Meccans were deeply hurt. They were not ones to take the defeat lying down. In 625, they organized an army of 3000 to take on Muhammad. This time too, Muhammad's army was outnumbered by around 3 times. But this war resulted in a stalemate. The Meccans failed to eliminate Muhammad.

In 627, around 10,000 soldiers were mobilized to take on Muhammad. To Muhammad there appeared no way of defeating them in a battle. So he thought of a novel way of defending his town. Medina was covered by hills on all the sides except one. On that side, he dug a trench to prevent the Meccan army from entering Medina. Such a strategy was never known in the entire Arabia. Meccans were shocked. They tried to cross the trench but failed. They waited outside for a fortnight before leaving.

As a result of these wars, Muhammad's reputation soared. More people came to believe that God must be on the side of Muslims and Muhammad must be the messenger of God.

What is of importance to the modern reader is that at a very early stage of the evolution of Islam, religion and politics got mixed up.

***

Though his military success enhanced his prestige, Muhammad had faced very serious internal problems in Medina. These problems came from the Jews. The pagans who didn't have any strong religion of their own, didn't find it difficult to accept Muhammad's leadership. But this was not the case with the Jews who had their own prophets, sacred texts and gods.

Muslims in the beginning were praying in the direction of Jerusalem like the Jews and Christians before them. But in 624, soon after the victory in the first battle, Muhammad changed the *qibla* (the direction of prayer). He asked the Muslims to pray in the direction of Mecca. This assertion of a new identity may have contributed to uneasy relationship of the Jews with Muhammad.

Muhammad had heard that some Jews were having secret meetings with the Meccans. He feared that their support to the Meccans would greatly weaken the defense of Medina. One clan of Jews was banished in 624; another one in 625. But worse was to happen to the Jews after the Trench war. Muhammad feared during the siege of Medina that the Jews might attack his army from inside and help the Meccans cross the trench.

The feared attack from the Jews didn't take place. But he thought banishing them would only help his enemies to become stronger. So he asked other leaders to decide what should be done to the Jews. And it was decided that all the able-bodied Jews should be oand women and children enslaved. Eight hundred Jews were beheaded – an event that was to have a permanent impact on the relations between the Jews and Muslims.

That the Jews had to be killed must have pained Muhammad. He was there at Medina to bring peace among the warring clans. Instead he brought wars and became responsible for the banishment of some of its people and killings of others.

Of course, it would be wrong to say that the Jews were killed because they were Jews. But it remains a fact that Muhammad failed to make the Jews feel secure under his leadership. His religion at a very early stage failed to integrate people of another religion that he himself respected.

But why do we take them as Jews at all and why not take them as just individuals who betrayed the people of their own town? They were accused collectively and punished collectively. So their identity as Jews is important. In fact, one can understand that it was their religious identity that prevented them from accepting Muhammad as their leader – unlike the pagans of Medina who had no strong religion of their own.

Was not beheading too cruel? No, not by the cultural standards then existing: treason was punished that way. Muhammad had tried banishment before but it did not work. By banishing them, he didn't want to add some more people to his list of enemies. That 10,000-strong army mobilized by the Meccans consisted of many tribes of Arabia.

But Jesus wouldn't have done that. The Buddha wouldn't have done that. Even Moses invoked the power of God to free the slaves from Egypt but norrt to kill any!

Yes, that is precisely how Muhammad is different from others. Jesus and the Buddha were specialists in religion. They had the luxury of such specialization because they were born in advanced civilizations. Muhammad was not a specialist in religion. He had to defend himself and his followers. He had to found a state out of warring tribes. He had to write a constitution, frame laws for the running of a state, raise an army and plan wars. The Buddha and Jesus were not doing tasks such as these.

God probably got sick of the specialists in religion. So he sent Muhammad – a complete man, who could kill when needed with the same spirit of righteousness that he prayed to God.

***

From a security point of view, Muhammad might be right in having betraying-Jews banished, killed or enslaved. But such actions make him more of a king and less of a messenger of God. Muhammad must have felt after the last war that he should put in all his efforts in winning over the Meccans and not in defeating them in a war.

In 628, with 1500 men Muhammad marched towards Mecca to make a pilgrimage. But Meccans barred his way. He signed a peace treaty with them. According to the treaty of al-Hudaybiya, Muhammad could make the pilgrimage but not in that year, but from the following year and every year for 10 more years. The draft of the treaty mentions Muhammad as 'messenger of God.' The Meccans objected to it, but the Muslims didn't want to yield. But Muhammad struck down the words 'messenger of God' and had himself mentioned simply as son of Abd-ullah — a compromise he considered worth making in the interest of peace.

In 629, Muhammad and his followers actually made the pilgrimage. But after the pilgrimage, there was some breach of treaty and Muhammad felt it was time to settle the issue with the Quraysh once for all. By this time, many in Mecca became Muslims. He marched towards Mecca with an army of 10,000. Quraysh saw no point in resisting the Muslim army. Muhammad offered general amnesty to one and all. The Ka'ba was cleared of all the pagan gods.

In 631, Muhammad made his last Hajj (Pilgrimage) when he gave his 'farewell sermon', in which he attempted to give the essence of his teaching. He asked the Muslims not to go astray from the path of righteousness after he was gone. He reminded them that each one would be answerable to God for one's deeds. He asked them to pay *zakat*, which is a portion of one's wealth, to the poor.

On women he said, "Remember you have taken them as wives only under God's trust and with His permission. Just as you have rights over them, they have rights over you."

He also said, "Be mindful of the people who work under you. Feed and clothe them as you feed and clothe yourselves."

On relations with other religions, he said, "Your Lord is one, and your father is one, all of you are from Adam. An Arab has no superiority over a non-Arab, except by piety and good action.

Treat others justly so that no one would be unjust to you. I leave behind two things, the Qur'an and my example and if you follow these, you will not fail."

Muhammad was ill for some time before he died in Medina on June 8th, 632.

***

Shari'a

Muhammad asked his disciples to follow his book as well as his life. This can be interpreted in a variety of ways.

The existing laws in the society he lived in were very primitive. Flogging, stoning, amputation and beheading were all considered a part of administering justice in that stateless society which had no jails. Muhammad always tried to make the laws just and humane.

Some female infants used to be left alone in a desert to die; this practice Muhammad banned outright.

As per the old law, women were not allowed to have a share in property. Muhammad recommended a share to them though only half of man's.

Slavery was the norm then. Muhammad didn't abolish slavery, but made freeing a slave a pious act.

The old law decreed that an adulterous woman should be stoned. Muhammad replaced stoning with lashing , that too only when four people had actually witnessed the intercourse, which is impossible!

The object of the changes he introduced was creation of a more just society.

However, missing the spirit of his reforms, some of his followers have misunderstood him in certain matters. Muhammad was living with his wives close to the mosque, a public place. To malign him, all sorts of charges were made against his wives. In a situation such as that, he asked his wives to cover themselves. That harmless instruction in the Qur'an gave ground to veiling, which is not covering but hiding themselves.

Modern societies are far advanced. To follow Muhammad now should mean more progressive legislation. It is certainly not in going back to those old systems of punishment in the name of *Shari'a* (The way to know God) – that Islamic law which was formulated during the 8th and 9th centuries on the basis of some instructions of the Qur'an, then existing laws of the primitive societies, and the *Hadiths* (actions and sayings of Muhammad as reported by others).

***

Sufism

It is not correct to think that thought-systems always degenerate in every aspect. Some innovations do take place. One such innovation is Sufism. This took place when Islam spread to distant lands and absorbed some of the best elements from the societies it had spread to.

Sufism is an innovation in the spiritual aspects of Islam. Muhammad would probably have been shocked by this innovation.

In the worldview of Muhammad, there is a huge gulf between the Creator and the created. The Qur'an mentions that Allah communicated to Muhammad in many indirect ways – through an angel, or from behind a veil, for example. There was not supposed to be a direct communication between mortals and Allah. Even a messenger is a mortal.

The Buddha proposed that in 'nirvana' there is communion with the whole world when the individual self is absent. The Bhakti tradition of Hinduism proposed the merger of the devotee with God. Islam is inspired by these ideas. The result is Sufism.

Through different ways, Sufis try to seek communion with Allah. And, interestingly, they maintain that Muhammad himself is a Sufi: it appeared to them that revelations were a result of beyond-ego processes.

When Islam spread, it did not spread simply as one moral code given in the Qur'an. It absorbed ideas from different sources and gave itself philosophical depth. Through such processes, it could win the respect even in the advanced societies.

***

Adaptation to secularism is more successful when one's religion is confined to spiritual aspects. Buddhism and Christianity confine themselves to spiritual aspects. Jesus emphasized that his kingdom was not that of the earth. The Buddha was born a prince, but renounced wealth as well as power. On the other hand, Muhammad was not a specialist. And Islamic life is not specialization. Muhammad proclaimed principles on many aspects of life. He was the political leader advocating those principles. All this meant that one's whole life is involved in Islam. So it is more difficult for the conservative Muslims to reduce religion to private sphere, what the Christians and the Buddhists can do with ease.

To the orthodox 'There is no god but Allah' implied 'There is no law, but Shari'a'. Also, the sacred details of Islam make it difficult for the conservative to be flexible towards the changing times.

***

Muhammad asked his disciples to follow his life as well as his teachings. But what was his life? His life provided an immense contrast to that of an orthodox Muslim. Muhammad was completely unorthodox, innovative and constantly experimenting.

It appears Muhammad held nothing as sacred till he was personally convinced or, in other words, till Allah revealed it to be so. His attitude towards marriage is a good example of this. His first wife, Khadija, was 15 years older than him. As long as she was alive, he didn't take anyone else as his wife. After her death he started marrying one after another. Some of his marriages are controversial. One of his wives was the divorced wife of his adopted son – this marriage had sparked protests then. At 53, he married his friend's daughter, a girl named A'isha – some say she was only 9 at the time of marriage, others put her age at 16. This girl went on to become his favorite wife. As part of building alliances with different tribes, Muhammad married many women – some say 9, some even 13. He then probably thought it was not right to marry so many, so he stopped marrying and asked others not to marry more than four.

Some now want to judge him whether each marriage of his was proper or not. What they miss is that Muhammad was constantly experimenting and trying to find out what was right and what was wrong.

He was founding not only a religion but a culture! No messenger ever dared try this.

No existing thing was sacred to him, for the sacred had to be revealed to him afresh.

***

Why was Muhammad against getting himself visually depicted? Why was Muhammad against Muslims making idols of him? He wanted Muslims to pray only to Allah and not any messenger. Messengers are only mediators. He was only a messenger.

Muhammad didn't want to be depicted as he was against taking the center-stage himself. There was no other reason for his opposition to being depicted. He was for the propagation of Islam, for the propagation of the Qur'an.

In this age of new communication media, would not a film depicting Muhammad in person spread his message to more number of people be desirable? It will surely not lead to worshipping of Muhammad. But this simple thing no one in the world dares – for fear of offending those claiming to be his followers.

***

Questions to think about

1. What do you know about the following?
   * Mecca, Ka'ba
   * Quraysh, 571 AD, Amina, Abu-Talib, Khadija
   * Mount Hira, 610 AD
   * Night Journey, Dome of Rock
   * Negus, Yathrib, Abu-Bakr, Ali, 622 AD
   * 624 AD at Badr, 625 AD, 627 AD
   * Beheading of 800 Jews, A'isha
   * 628 AD, treaty of al-Hudaybiya, 629 AD
   * Farewell sermon, 632 AD

2. What are the central tenets of Islam?

3. What do the following mean?
   * Qur'an, Islam, Salat, Medina, Hijra, Ummah, Hajj
   * Qibla, zakat, sharia, Hadiths

4. Who are 'people of the book'?

5. What is meant by constitution of Medina?

6. What are Islam's unique elements?
   * Link between religion and politics
   * Role of warfare
   * Building culture

7. What in your view are the differences between Jesus and Muhammad?

17. Jesus Christ

The main source of the story of Jesus is based on the New Testament. The four gospels of Matthew, Mark, Luke and John constitute a major part of the New Testament. These gospels were written around the first century. Mark's is considered the earliest, written around 40 years after the death of Jesus. Historians use the events and people mentioned in these gospels to verify the historicity of the account.

The gospels narrate the story of Jesus to show that he is a son of God – around that time only Roman emperors could claim such divine parenthood. The gospels also meant to show that he was Christ – means 'the anointed' or the messiah. He was the long-awaited Jewish messiah as mentioned in the Old Testament. He was supposed to be the son of David, who was the first divinely approved king of Israel as per the Old Testament. His ancestry was traced to Abraham. This is how Jesus, son of a humble carpenter (or a builder), is given divine ancestry.

His birth itself is presented as a miracle. His life is full of miracles. And he is said to have come back to life after his death and ascended to heaven.

Jesus was born around the beginning of the first century AD. He was born to Mary, who was then betrothed to Joseph – both living in Nazareth, Galilee. Mary was supposed to be a virgin who conceived Jesus through Holy Spirit. Through Angel Gabriel, Mary and Joseph were informed of this plan of God.

When Mary was about to give birth, she and Joseph travelled to Bethlehem. In a census, citizens were asked to register their names in their ancestral places. It was in Bethlehem that Jesus was born. This had been an important town in the Old Testament. It was the native place of David's father. David was anointed king there. Anyway, a ruler was supposed to come from Bethlehem. Because they could not get accommodation in an inn, Mary had to deliver her baby in a manger.

Following a star, three wise men (also called Magi, which means astrologers) bring gifts to Jesus and declare him to be the king of Jews. This star too is as per the predictions of the Old Testament. Shepherds too get to know of this great event and come to visit the new baby.

Gospels inform us that Herod the Great, the king of Judea – which was then a client kingdom within the Roman empire – learnt that a king of Jews had been born. Fearing that his rival was just born, he ordered that all the newborn male children be put to death – exactly like what Pharaoh did to Moses and Kamsa to Krishna. Unlike Holy Spirit or Gabriel, Herod was a historical figure, but his infanticide was not reported in any historical source. As per the gospels, the angel warns Joseph to flee to Egypt to save the child. So they flee and return later to settle in Nazareth. Talking of prophecies, one of God's sons was expected to come from Egypt.

Thus, the messiah was born as prophesied in the Old Testament. That Jesus of Nazareth was Christ. This is the point made in the gospels.

***

John the Baptist

John the Baptist was a very important figure in the life of Jesus. There is historical evidence to suggest that John was a popular preacher. He had thousands of followers. John was critical of Herod's marrying his brother's former wife, which is a violation of the rules of the Old Testament. Herod not only disliked John's criticism of him but also feared his popularity. Herod imprisoned John and finally executed him.

What was John preaching then? He had been saying that a messiah would come. Jesus was to claim later that he was that messiah. In that way John prepared the way for Jesus. The idea of repenting for sins was John's. He was baptizing people, which involved their taking a ritual bath in a holy river seeking pardon for the sins (similar to Hindus' ritual bath in the Ganga).

According to the gospels, Jesus came from Nazareth to be baptized by John in the Jordan river. Then a miracle happened at the time of baptism. When Jesus came out of the waters, a voice from the sky proclaimed that Jesus was God's son. According to the gospels, Jesus began his ministry only after the execution of John by Herod.

John was taken as the last messiah of the Old Testament and the first messiah of the New Testament. Interestingly, according to the Qur'an, on his way to heaven, Prophet Muhammad met John along with Jesus!

Some say that the importance of John was downplayed by gospel writers and the early Christians to show Jesus in a better light. It need not be viewed that way. The boldness of Jesus was that he claimed that he was the messiah, whereas John was waiting for the arrival of a messiah. In fact, in making himself the long-awaited messiah, Jesus made John too an important figure. According to the Old Testament, one was supposed to be sent to announce the arrival of Messiah. That status was conferred on John by Jesus himself.

***

Sermon on the Mount as given in Matthew's gospel is considered to be the essence of the teachings of Jesus. What he spoke then was undoubtedly a huge advancement over the ethics preached before. Let us see the central points he made:

- 'The blessed are you, the poor,' Jesus said. 'The blessed are you the hungry now, ' he said. The kingdom of heaven is theirs. Jesus stood for the weak.

- And against the privileged. 'Woe to you who are rich. You have received your consolation' 'Woe to you who are full now. You shall be hungry.'

- The earlier morality was against bad actions. But Jesus was against thoughts as well. If you are angry you are unfavorably judged. So is a lustful thought!

- And love your enemy. Pray for your persecutors. If one strikes you on one cheek, offer him the other. Earlier morality advocated helping friends and harming enemies.

- If you give charity don't announce it to everyone. If

you are praying, don't announce to everyone that you are doing so. All good things are watched by God. No one else needs to know.

Mahatma Gandhi was greatly influenced by this sermon. He stood for the poor. He wanted to purify his mind. He evolved the technique of non-violent struggle. And his prayer was an intensely personal affair with God.

How would the Buddha differ with the message of Jesus? The Buddha stood for kindness. And he thought love should be offered in response to hatred. He was also for purification of the mind. But to the Buddha, there was no God – so no Father to watch and reward later. More importantly, all this is only secondary to the final goal of bliss.

In fact, with or without God to watch, we know love has the power to dent hate, though it may not eliminate it in every case. Gandhi believed that since there is truth in every human, love has the capacity to transform anyone.

Surely in his advocacy of love, Jesus preached a highly advanced moral principle rooted in real human nature.

Did his teachings have a political meaning? Jesus was talking about the kingdom of heaven, but that kingdom was not unrelated to the kingdom on the earth. The poor here would be blessed there. The rich here would be punished there. In effect he was saying that the system on the earth was evil. He saw the existing system as unfair – not unlike the way Marx would view.

***

Jesus performed many miracles in his lifetime. People around him who were supposed to have witnessed these miracles believed that he was indeed the son of God.

Once during a party, when wine was over, Jesus turned water into wine. When an official approached Jesus saying that his son was about to die, Jesus said 'your son would live' and his son was cured. Jesus restored vision to the one born-blind. Once, when thousands of followers arrived and there was not enough food, Jesus produced all the food required from a few loaves of bread. He made the disabled walk. Once Jesus brought back to life someone who had been buried four days ago. Once he walked on water. On another occasion, he even calmed a storm.

***

The last week of the life of Jesus occupies one-third of the narrative in the gospels. It starts with Jesus entering Jerusalem.

Jesus asks his disciples to get a young donkey to ride. As per the Old Testament, the messiah was supposed to enter Jerusalem on a donkey! Jesus was enacting that role, or announcing his status to everyone! He went on as crowds cheered him.

What antagonized the Jewish authorities was Jesus' criticism of activities in a holy temple. When Jesus saw money-changers in the temple, he angrily drove them out declaring that a place meant for prayer could not be a den of thieves. He then started preaching in the temple, which the authorities did not approve of.

They wanted to fix him as a political rebel deserving death. They wanted to depict him as somebody inciting people not to pay taxes. But Jesus always claimed that his mission was only religious, not political. In response to a question, he said 'Render to Caesar the things that are Caesar's and to God the things that are God's.' This statement was later construed to mean separation of religion from politics.

The authorities nevertheless decided to punish him. They only had to decide on what charge.

***

The Last Supper is the final meal Jesus had with his twelve disciples. Anticipating that would be his last meeting, he did many unusual things. He broke a loaf of bread and gave pieces to them saying that it was his body. He gave them wine saying that was his blood. He washed everyone's feet after the supper. Jesus said, 'one of you will betray me.' To Peter he said, 'You will deny three times this night any knowledge of me.'

After that supper, Jesus went for a walk. While he was in the garden of Gethsemane, he saw Judas coming with Jewish priests and some other people with weapons. Judas approached Jesus and kissed him, as a way of identifying him to the authorities. Jesus was then arrested. When one of the disciples tried to defend him by a sword Jesus prevented him, saying 'all who live by the sword shall die by the sword'.

***

Jesus was first put on trial before a Jewish council and then taken to Pontius Pilate who sent him to Herod Antipas saying the Galilean should be tried by him. Jesus said nothing to Herod's questions. So he was sent back to Pilate.

Jewish elders charged that Jesus was claiming that he was the king of Jews. Jesus said that his kingdom was not of the earth. In the end Pilate found Jesus innocent. But the crowd insisted on punishment. Pilate then ordered Jesus' crucifixion, even while saying 'I am innocent of this man's blood.'

After the trial, Jesus was handed over to Roman soldiers. The soldiers beat him and mocked him as the King of Jews by placing a crown of thorns on his head. He was then sent to Calvary for crucifixion.

Along the way he told the women crying not to cry for him but for themselves and their children. Jesus was crucified between two convicted criminals. Jesus refused to take a painkiller when offered. Above his head was the inscription *King of the Jews*. Before dying he said 'Father, forgive them for they know not what they are doing.'

Crucifixion was not mentioned in the prophecies of the Old Testament. The messiah was not supposed to die as a convicted criminal.

***

Following his death on Friday, Jesus' body was removed from the cross that evening, with the permission of Pilate. It was then wrapped in a clean cloth and buried in a new tomb. But then on Sunday the tomb was discovered to be empty.

The resurrected Jesus first appeared to Mary Magdalene and later to others. Jesus made a series of appearances before ascending to heaven forty days after his resurrection.

♦ ♦ ♦ ♦ ♦ ♦

Questions to think about

1. What do you know about the following?
   * Old Testament, New Testament
   * Matthew, Mark, Luke and John
   * Gospels
   * Meaning of Christ
   * King David
   * Mary, Joseph, Holy Spirit, Gabriel
   * Nazareth, Galilee, Bethlehem, Judea
   * Magi
   * Herod
   * John the Baptist
   * Baptism

2. Do you agree with the following?
   * "The blessed are you, the poor."
   * "The blessed are you, the hungry."
   * "Woe to you who are full now. You shall be hungry."
   * "Woe to you who are rich. You have received your

consolation."

3. What did Gandhi learn from the message of Jesus?

4. What do you know about the following?
   - Jerusalem in the time of Jesus
   - Last Supper
   - Peter, Judas, Gethsemane
   - Pontius Pilate
   - Crucifixion
   - Resurrection
   - Mary Magdalene
   - Ascent to heaven

5. What is the meaning of the following?
   "Render unto Caesar the things that are Caesar's and
   unto God the things that are God's"

6. Should not evil be returned with evil? What happens if it
   is returned?

7. Is it possible to return evil with love? If not possible,
   what is the next best course of action?

8. What is Gandhi's notion of Truth?

9. Should a person believe in God for him to have Truth
   inside?

10. What is the essence of man – evil or truth?

11. If hate is responded with love, how is that supposed to
    transform hate?

12. Is not responding with hate necessary in
    administration?

13. How do these people claim to know truth? How did
    they choose to communicate it?

- Socrates, Jesus, Buddha, Gandhi, Marx

14. How does self-knowledge discourage hate-based approach?

15. What is common to the death of Socrates, Jesus and Gandhi?

16. Do the poor deserve to be the poor? What would Jesus say? What would Marx say?

18. Gautam Buddha

Siddhartha, whose family name was Gotama, lived in the 6th century BC in north India. His father, Suddhodana, was the ruler of the kingdom of Sakyas. He was born at Lumbini (now in Nepal). His mother, Maya, died a week after his birth. At the age of 16 years, he married Yasodhara. At the age of 29 years, he left his kingdom, after the birth of his only child Rahula.

It was under a fig tree, since then called Bodhi-tree (tree of wisdom), on the banks of the Neranjara river, near Gaya, at the age of 35 years, that he attained enlightenment. After that he was called the Buddha, The Enlightened One. He gave his first sermon to five of his old colleagues in Deer Park, at Sarnath, near Benares. He taught for 45 years and passed away at the age of 80 years at Kusinara, in Uttar Pradesh. His teachings were orally passed on till the 1st century BC, when they were put in a written form.

***

According to the life story of the Buddha, when he was born, scholars predicted that he would either be a great king or a great religious figure. His father wanted him to be a great king. He was advised that Siddhartha should never know suffering for then he would not be drawn to religion. So Siddhartha was exposed to only pleasure. He was not free to leave the palace and see the world.

The story goes that Siddhartha did leave the palace on a few occasions. On one occasion, he came across a sick man. Then he understood sickness. On another occasion, he saw an old man. Then he understood old age. On yet another occasion, he saw a dead man. Then he understood death. Thus he understood that life is full of inevitable sorrow. Then he came across a monk who had renounced everything and was in search of truth. Then the Buddha thought he too should renounce worldly life to find an end to suffering.

We are told that the Buddha found solution to human sorrow under the Bodhi tree at Gaya. But he did not find any solution to sickness. He did not find any solution to ageing. Nor did he find anything by which man can defy death. As years passed, the Buddha became old and aged and suffered from many ailments. In the end, he died of food poisoning – his enlightenment didn't even help him recognize that food was unhealthy!

It was said that before sitting under that tree, Siddhartha told himself, 'I will not leave this place till I find the solution.' What was it that convinced him that he had found the solution to sorrow?

***

The philosophy of the Buddha is often summarized in *four noble truths*. The first noble truth is that there is *dukkha*. The second noble truth deals with the origin of dukkha: That it comes from thirst – various kinds of desires. The third noble truth is that this thirst can be ended. The fourth noble truth tells us the means of ending this thirst. It gives us an *eight-fold path* by which desires can be ended and what the Buddha attained can be attained by others.

The eight-fold path puts us on the way to nirvana. It tells us what we should be doing if we are serious about *nirvana* – that is enlightenment. We should have (1) right understanding: we should correctly understand what the Buddha is teaching – not just at the superficial level, but at a deeper level. We should have (2) right thought. We should have thoughts of love and detachment. We should (3) speak rightly. We should abstain from uttering lies, slander and gossip. We should (4) act rightly. We should not steal, engage in dishonest action, or have illegitimate sex. We should have (5) right livelihood. We should not choose professions that involve harming others. We should put in (6) right effort to have a quiet state of mind and clear our mind of all impurities. We should develop (7) right mindfulness. That is, we should be aware of our sensations, feelings and thoughts. We should develop (8) right concentration. We should focus attention on the physical and psychological aspects of our living.

Buddhist teaching is also called the *Middle Path*. It avoided extremes of asceticism and indulgence in sensory pleasures. According to the story, Siddhartha first approached religious teachers popular at that time. Under their instructions, he did various exercises. He deprived the body of its needs and pleasures. Before sitting under the Bodhi tree, he was on the verge of death. A woman gave him some food which helped him to survive. He had been taught that by body deprivation, he could control the mind and by controlling the mind he could eliminate sorrow. The Buddha realized that neither body deprivation nor its indulgence takes one closer to truth.

***

Suppose one speaks truth and doesn't steal or do bad things. How is that supposed to end sorrow when one is fired from one's job? One also observes the mind and understands oneself. One also concentrates on something like breathing. One may also have a less noisy mind. But how is that supposed to end sorrow once for all?

More importantly, what is this business of ending sorrow without being free from sickness, ageing and death, the issues that are supposed to have driven Siddhartha out of the palace?

***

He did say that if one makes it to nirvana in this birth, one will not have rebirth. If one is not going to be born, one will not suffer. Surely that is not a very elegant solution to sorrow! Moreover, if nirvana makes one free from sorrow in this birth, why should one avoid rebirth? One can seek rebirth and using nirvana one will be free from sorrow in the new birth too.

In the light of advancement of science, the idea of rebirth or freedom from rebirth is the silliest thing the Buddha taught. If sitting under that tree was giving him truth, he should have sat there for some more time to get rid of such silly ideas!

Perhaps rebirth is the only idea of the Buddha that modern man of science can reject. The Buddha rejected the idea of God.

He rejected the idea of heaven and hell – thereby rejecting the very idea of divine supervision and divine judgment in the end. There are no supernatural reasons why man should be good.

He rejected the idea of soul – that immortal, unchanging thing, ever present across various births – though be believed in rebirth. One's actions lead to their logical consequences – even across births! The actions are not divinely judged and rewarded.

Drunken driving reduces your attentiveness and increases the possibility of accidents; God has no role in this matter. No

external agency is posited. The lesson is this: do not drink and drive. Also, don't think that you can get over the problem of inattentiveness by bribing god or pleasing Him.

The Buddha did not claim that he was different in any way. He was like any other human being. Having rejected the idea of God, one can't claim to be God's son, or God's messenger. His teaching is not a result of any revelation.

Nor did the Buddha say that his teaching should be accepted blindly. He said he should be accepted only to the extent he is understood.

Admiring him, worshipping him doesn't bring any merit. If statues are made for him, temples are constructed for him and if rituals and ceremonies are performed by his disciples, it is despite what he taught. Since people are used to the idea of god, they made him a god and worshipped him as god. It is *their* approach to sorrow, not his.

Even in terms of social ideals, he was far ahead of his time. He rejected the caste system when discrimination on the basis of caste and occupation on the basis of caste was part of religious duty then.

Fine, he may be as logical and as modern as David Hume. But how about his claim to knowing the solution to sorrow? The Buddha should be judged by that – the issue of sorrow is central to his search as well as his claimed solution.

***

Walpola Rahula, a Buddhist monk and scholar, in his *What the Buddha Taught* states four noble truths in terms of *dukkha* – he does not translate the term into its ordinary meaning 'suffering' or 'sorrow'. He says the Buddha's reference to *dukkha* has at least three distinct meanings.

The first level of meaning is that dukkha means sorrow/ suffering – the sense in which it is ordinarily used. The second level of meaning refers even to pleasures that in future bring pain. As of now they are pleasures, but soon they are very likely to bring pain. Continuing the same example, drinking before driving is pleasure with pain in-built. These two levels are easy to understand.

And there is the third level. This refers to certain states of conditioning. It refers to some kind of sticking to something that is impermanent… or some such thing. This third level is seen as the source of sorrow of the first two kinds.

In effect, the Buddha is saying the source of sorrow is not external. Events happen – sickness happens, ageing happens, death happens. Such events cause sorrow because we have, in some very important ways, distorted understanding of ourselves. If those distortions are removed the same events don't produce suffering – as we know it.

We can say the Buddha went all prepared to find a way out of suffering. To his shock, he found there was no suffering to be overcome!

But what are the distortions we have that cause suffering? This modern psychology should investigate. But what should it focus on? What should it try to study? What would the Buddha suggest?

Considerable evidence suggests that the research should be on the nature of self, i.e. the sense of 'I'. The Buddha seems to be suggesting that the sense of 'I' is not based on the correct perception. Realization of *Anatta* (no-self) is a very important thing, according to him.

Modern research need not bank only on the Buddha's teachings. Walpola Rahula who was very familiar with J. Krishnamurti's teachings and who also had wide-ranging discussions with him said that Krishnamurti's teaching was "practically the same" as the Buddha's. So Krishnamurti literature can help.

***

So what the Buddha said remains to be decoded. It remains to be understood. And the social implications of his teachings remain to be examined. Buddhism thus belongs to the future – all other religions belong to the past.

Buddha: Morality is not the end. It is only an intelligent companion in one's journey towards the bliss.

Religions are equal only at a basic level – be kind, be good, do not murder. At a higher level, they are different. So the idea of essential oneness of religions or their equality is not true. Since truth is degenerating into group identity, the idea of equality is promoted to encourage tolerance.

Buddhism is by far the most advanced. The modern man is yet to decipher it.

♦ ♦ ♦

Questions to think about

1. What do you know about the following?
   * Siddhartha, Sakyas, Lumbini, Yasodhara
   * Niranjana river, Gaya
   * Deer Park, Sarnath
   * Kusinara, UP

2. What are the four noble truths?

3. What is an eightfold path?

4. What is Middle Path?

5. What is Buddha's solution to sorrow?

6. What can you say about how religions are founded?

7. Are all religions equally valid?

8. What do you know about Sufism?

19. Ramakrishna Paramahamsa

"He who was Rama and He who was Krishna is now Ramakrishna in this body," Ramakrishna Paramahamsa (1833-86) was reported to have told his favourite disciple Swami Vivekananda in the last stage of his life. That was a claim that he was Divinity itself.

How can a man in flesh and blood make such a claim?

Yes, that is possible in Hinduism, only in Hinduism. Jesus claimed he was son of God, Muhammad claimed he was a prophet but in Hinduism a man can claim he is God himself. How is it possible?

The idea is that man has a separative consciousness and when this ends he becomes one with God. Put differently, he becomes God. Ramakrishna of the 19th century is only a recent illustration of the mystical religious tradition of ancient India.

There are two things that Ramakrishna was known for: trances and visions. We do not scientifically know what exactly a trance – also called Samadhi – is. We only know that a person loses the consciousness of his body and the surroundings.

Ramakrishna experienced this for the first time when he was only six. While walking along the paddy fields in his village in Bengal, he saw a sedge of white cranes flying against dark clouds and got so absorbed in watching them that he lost consciousness and experienced a state of bliss. Later he had such trances while worshipping gods.

Ramakrishna was also famous for having visions of various gods. He was reported to have had a vision of Kali when working as a priest at Dakshineswar Kali Temple. These visions were not confined to Kali; he had visions of many other gods – even Jesus and Muhammad!

Having had visions of many gods, he began teaching that God is real and various paths lead to God. He taught, "Different creeds are but different paths to reach the Almighty,[1]" and "A truly religious man should think that other religions also are paths leading to the truth."

Based on his experience of feeling oneness with God, he said, "When egoism drops away, Divinity manifests itself."

How should one drop one's ego? To Ramakrishna, worldly desires are a hindrance to god-realization. "General rule is that no one can attain spiritual perfection unless he renounces lust and greed." He worshipped even his wife Sarada Devi as a goddess. He used to throw coins along with stones into the river saying the two were of equal value.

The worldly desires should go, and in their place spiritual desires should manifest. "Desires of holiness, devotion and love are not to be reckoned as desires at all." "He is truly a pious man who is dead even in life, that is, whose passions and desires

---

1. All the quotations except the first one in this lesson are taken from
  Ramakrishna: His Life and Sayings by Max Muller.

have been all but destroyed as in a dead body."

The spiritual goals are to be pursued with a sense of self-confidence. "If you think yourself to be morally weak and without goodness, you will really find yourself to be so in no time. Know and believe that you are of immense power, and the power will come to you at last."

Evaluation

1. Efforts to control lust may actually increase the passion rather than reduce it.

2. Spiritual desires are also desires. Ramakrishna didn't consider the problems associated with the spiritual desires, as K did.

3. Gods he was having visions of, are only man's creations. So his experience (or his interpretation of it) is somewhere adulterated – unlike Ramana Maharshi's which did not have to include human inventions like gods.

    According to some accounts, a monk by name Totapuri tried to convince Ramakrishna of this but did not succeed.

♦ ♦ ♦

***Totapuri:** Ramakrishna, move over Kali and all other conceptual forms and see the formless infinity.*

◆ ◆ ◆

Questions to think about

1. Describe the spiritual experiences of Ramakrishna Paramahamsa.

2. Why did he come to believe that different religions are only different paths to God?

3. What is his stand on self-control? Do you endorse it?

4. What do you think about his obsession with Kali?

20. Swami Vivekananda

If a good student is the one who rectifies, refines, updates and modifies what his teacher has taught, then Swami Vivekananda (1863-1902) is not a good student of Ramakrishna Paramahamsa. Vivekananda found no fault with his master; he only had unflinching admiration for him. "Judge him not through me, I am only a weak instrument[1]," Vivekananda said.

Narendra Nath – his name before he became a monk – started his life as a rational and sceptical man. He read the works of Hume, Kant, Hegel, Schopenhauer, Comte, Spencer, Mill and Darwin. He even translated Spencer's *Education* into Bengali. But he always had an urge to lead a religious life. He shocked many by asking, 'Have you seen God?' No one could satisfy his rational approach to religion – till he met Ramakrishna.

When Narendra asked Ramakrishna, 'Have you seen God?' he answered, 'Yes, of course, but more clearly than I see you now.' Under Ramakrishna, Narendra's scepticism gave place to deep belief in religious phenomena.

---

1. All the quotations taken from the film *Vivekananda by Vivekananda*

In a way Ramakrishna produced Swami Vivekananda out of Narendra Nath. How did he accomplish this? First, by recognising the greatness in Narendra Nath. "It was his unflinching trust in me and love that bound me to him for ever." This trust, "even my mother and brother did not have." Ramakrishna would say, "Naren, you are a hero. The very sight inspires me with courage."

Trust in Narendra's competence was not the only thing. Ramakrishna loved Narendra very much. Narendra was born in a rich family, but after his father's death his family faced many financial troubles that disturbed him. When Ramakrishna heard of Narendra's troubles, he said, "For your sake I could beg from door to door." "He tamed me with his love," said Vivekananda.

What did Ramakrishna want Vivekananda to do? Interestingly, it was not going through trances and having visions. When Vivekananda once said, I want to go into Samadhi for 4 or 5 days, Ramakrishna said, "Are you not ashamed? You are interested in your small experiences; you are meant for big things."

What were those big things that Vivekananda was expected to achieve?

***

Vivekananda's teaching read outside the historical context appears rather silly. "Arise, awake, stop not till the goal is reached," is like that cheap ambition-provoking stuff. To that add patriotism, "the very dust of India has become holy to me. The very air is holy." He offers a recipe for producing narrow-minded and aggressive patriots.

But in the context in which it was delivered, Vivekananda's message was divine. What was the context?

Ramakrishna showed how man can meet God. But he showed it to the Indians who forgot they were humans at all. In other words, Ramakrishna gave a message to the people humbled, humiliated and feeling inferior. To the people who had no sense of self-worth, no sense of pride, no sense of dignity.

For self to merge with God, it should first have a sense of dignity. It is this dignity that Vivekananda attempted to instil in the Indians. He showed that Hindus need not be ashamed of their past; their religion is not inferior to any; and they were a great people once and they can make a great nation now.

In 1893, at the Parliament of World Religions in Chicago, Vivekananda proclaimed to the world how Hinduism has taught the world both tolerance and universal acceptance. He said Hinduism believed that different religions were different ways to reach God "as the different streams having their sources in different places all mingle their water in the sea." America was stunned by his interpretation of Hinduism, his eloquence and the power of his message. When Herald News wrote, "How foolish it is to send missionaries to this learned nation," Vivekananda made his point, Hinduism made its point, India made its point. It was a revelation for Indians that their religion was not inferior to any.

Vivekananda's sense of pride did not blind him to the evils in the Hindu society: the caste system, illiteracy, poverty, and ill-treatment of women. He wanted Indians to work for the removal of these evils. When he provoked ambition in men, it was never for glorification of self or for acquisition of material things but for the nobler cause of building a great nation. He said monks should work for the removal of social evils without wasting time on debating on vague metaphysical issues. Vivekananda's concern for the wellbeing of Indians inspired many Indians. "After reading his works, my love for the country became a thousand-fold," said Gandhi.

Vivekananda lived to make Ramakrishna's great message more relevant to the humbled nation. In fact, instead of thinking that Vivekananda died young it is more sensible to think that Ramakrishna lived through Vivekananda 16 years longer to make his teaching more appropriate to the context.

◆ ◆ ◆

Questions to think about

1. How was Vivekananda influenced by Ramakrishna Paramahamsa?

2. What is the significance of Parliament of World Religions, 1893?

3. Summarize the teachings of Vivekananda. How significant were they during his times?

21. Ramana Maharshi

Ramana Maharshi (1879-1950) was born in Tiruchuzhi, some 30 miles from Madurai in Tamil Nadu. He was named Venkataraman Iyer. One unusual trait of his, which he revealed later, was that when he slept, he was so completely lost in sleep that his friends could beat him without waking him up. When he was 11, he was sent to study at Dundigal, his uncle's place, to receive education in English. Later he moved to Madurai when his uncle moved to that place. When his father died in 1892, for some time the boy contemplated death.

In 1895, he read Periyapuranam, a book that describes the lives of 63 Saivite saints. He was deeply moved by their lives. He began to make devotional visits to the Meenakshi Temple in Madurai.

In 1896, when he was 17 years old, he had a life-changing experience. He narrated this experience in 1930 over a series of conversations. He said he had been seized with the fear of death. He then proceeded to inquire what would happen after death. He enacted his death experience – all senses stopped.

Then he felt awareness of something large – beyond body and mind. What he realized that day remained with him forever. Ramana later called this death experience 'sudden liberation' as opposed to 'gradual liberation' that some others may experience.

He could no longer take an interest in studies and in relationships. A few weeks after that event, he left his house leaving a note, taking a part of the money he had been given to pay the college fees. He traveled to Tiruvannamalai. He never moved out of it for the rest of his life.

He lived in temples there before moving to caves in Arunachala hill in 1899 where he lived till 1922. From then onwards till his death he lived in what is now Ramana Ashramam at the foot of the hill.

It was a Vedic scholar, Ganapati Sastri, who proclaimed him as Bhagwan Sri Ramana Maharshi in 1907.

***

"What we find in the life and teachings of Sri Ramana is the purest of India. He is the whitest spot in a white space," wrote Jung, the psychologist who had an extensive knowledge of religious and mystical traditions of the East and the West.

India did a lot of white. Sri Ramana is only the whitest spot in a white space. Jung rejected taking Ramana "as an isolated phenomenon."

Indian philosophy – generated in the religions of Hinduism or Buddhism all through these centuries – has many, many theories and beliefs. If we leave all that is unnecessary or superstitious and try to take the very best, it will, most probably, be more or less what Ramana taught.

So, what did he teach? Can it be compared with that of other religious figures, or social scientists?

What he said is not in the realm of words and ideas, but of experience. So we can't explain the way we explained others. What we can try to figure out is what he may be pointing out. We can also go around his teaching – reflecting on what he is not saying.

***

If one has practiced many wrong things before realizing truth, then one will go about saying what those wrong things are. That will be helpful to seekers. The Buddha is an example of this. But Ramana didn't do such things before his 'death experience', which is now called self-realization.

If one is a well-read person, then one will be able to compare his knowledge with that of others. He can explain how his is different from others. But Ramana is not a knowledgeable person.

This is a case of a teenager accidentally hitting on Truth. It is only after realizing the Truth that he makes sense of it, understands its rarity and tries to explain it to others.

It is said he communicates his wisdom through silence! It can't be otherwise. He had never passed through the states of confusion that others are in to verbalize his Truth.

It is also said that he speaks directly. Such directness comes from knowing only what he has realized and nothing more.

In a nutshell, he didn't deliver lectures. His teaching consists of brief conversations with the people who came to visit him. They are in the question-and-answer mode. He said almost nothing other than what was extracted out of him. A deeper question does elicit a deeper answer.

But whatever one asks, however deep it is, however fundamental it is, however specific it is, he will answer. He will answer in a way that shocks the questioner. The answers are very insightful and terse. The examples or analogies are completely fresh and unusual. It is clear that he is not speaking from any book or others' knowledge, but only from what he has realized.

Also one notices that behind those shockingly diverse answers, there is one point he has been trying to convey. Whatever be the question, his answer in fact appears to be the only one. Whatever be the question, he has been trying to say the same thing – again and again.

Ramana has only one point – no noble truths, no eight-fold path.

So what is that point?

***

In terms of traditional Indian classification, Ramana's teaching is an example of Jnanamarg – method of insightful reflection and inquiry into the nature of mind. Ramana's method is called the method of self-inquiry.

But what is this self-enquiry? Is it the same thing as 'know thyself?' Is this what Socrates asked us to do? A very, very emphatic 'No.' Socrates wants us to examine our life – the way we think, the way we relate to – that gives us happiness. He wants us to act rationally and justly. Ramana is not concerned about this.

Then, is it similar to Freud's idea that we delve deep into

our unconscious? Should we probe our fears, dreams, childhood influences, our urges and conflicting moral codes? Again an emphatic 'No'. Ramana is least concerned.

Socrates and Freud want us to understand the ways of self so that we can behave more rationally, more intelligently and lead lives with less conflict. But Ramana is not talking about that.

Ramana's inquiry is not regarding how self works, but regarding its source. It is about the origin of self – not about types of self: happy self, unhappy self, good self, bad self, kind self, unkind self.

Ramana wants us to inquire into the source of self – how it emerges and not what it does once it emerges. It is something that emerges – there is no self in deep sleep. Even during wakefulness, it appears and disappears.

This self has certain properties: It does certain things in certain ways; it seeks pleasure and sometimes succeeds but often ends up with pain; it helps others; it also harms some; it wants to purify itself; it wants to accumulate religious merit which it does sometimes but it also sins. These are the ways of self.

However healthy a self is, however integrated it is, self is constantly balancing. It will never succeed in avoiding what it wants to avoid. It can never avoid pain. It can never avoid conflict. However much one understands self, that understanding doesn't free one from the self.

So Ramana is solely concerned with the source of self.

***

Then, is not this the same thing that the Buddha taught?

'Probably,' that is why Ramana is not an isolated phenomenon.

140

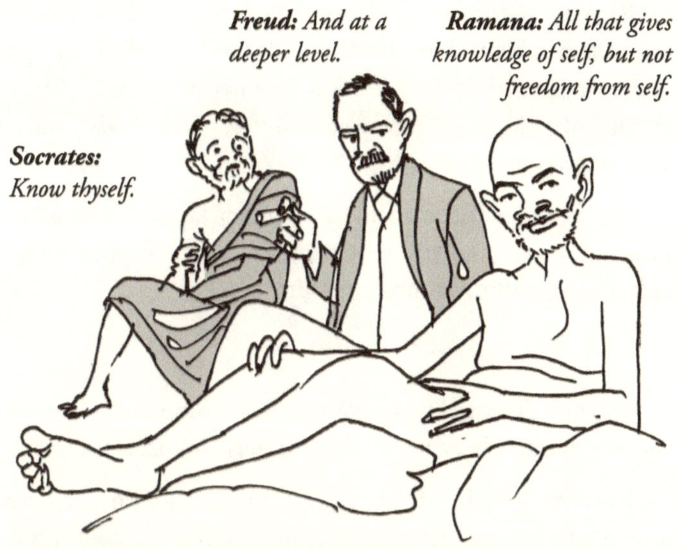

Is this whiter than the Buddha's?

'Probably, Right livelihood, right speech, right concentration..' all that stuff is cut off. Take up smuggling as livelihood if you want. Murder a few. But just sit down and see who is doing all that. If you can arrive at the source, it is all over.

Even realization of sorrow is not necessary to reach Truth. The Buddha's central question has been how to end sorrow. Ramana says coolly he learnt from others that there normally is much sorrow in life!

The Buddha does say that what he has been asking his disciples to practice – like eight-fold path – is only a raft that will help them go to a different shore, but truth is not the raft. The eight-fold path does give the impression that the journey is long. Ramana cuts short the journey. Self-realization can be immediate – and possible for anyone.

Ramana didn't believe in purifying the mind; impurities are an inevitable part of the mind. Nor did he believe in right concentration – wavering is in the very nature of the mind. He would only ask us again and again 'why do you identify yourself with that mind?'

The Buddha added to his core understanding – which is possibly no different from Ramana's – a lot of other things. Ramana kept things simple and direct.

***

Yet, not all would agree with the said comparison between the Buddha and Ramana – for some very important reasons.

Ramana's mode of teaching is that he doesn't criticize any method, any practice. If one says, 'I want to concentrate on breathing', he will say 'fine, after that find out who is

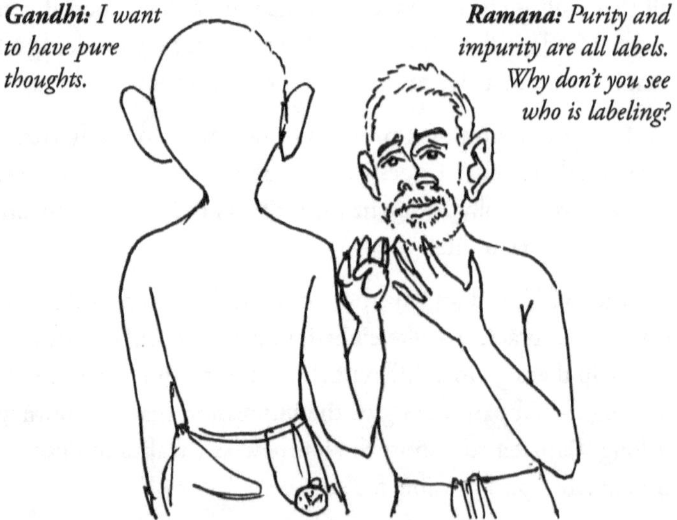

concentrating.' He gives his method without criticizing any. One has one's own version of Ramana.

Nor did he look at religion as an intellectual, as a purely rational being – which I think the Buddha did. The Buddha did away with so many useless concepts, criticized the past. Lots of cleansing he did. That religious cleansing had social and political consequences. Ramana made no such attempt. In his name, any rubbish can get through.

To many Hindus, he is just a saint, worshipping whom may even lead to material benefits. They miss the radicalism of his teaching. Today's Ramana Ashramam at Tiruvannamalai is temple-like. Many truths get degenerated into rituals. But in the case of Ramana, that process was very fast.

No wonder, the Buddha founded a religion whereas Ramana ended being a deity in an old religion. But on that count, Ramana should have no regrets – after all no religion is founded on the basis of an accident.

◆ ◆ ◆

Questions to think about

1. What do you know about Ramana's death experience?

2. What is Ramana's central message?

3. How would he look at the Gandhian type of self-control?

4. How would he look at Socratic type of self-knowledge?

5. How would he look at sorrow as the means for realization?

22. Mahatma Gandhi

Mahatma Gandhi (1869 – 1948) showed to the world how an evil can be transformed by sheer moral force. Gandhi proved on a bigger scale the power of what Jesus had taught.

His politics revolved around the principle, 'There is truth in everyman and it can be ignited by a moral force.' During his fight against the British Empire in South Africa, he evolved many of his methods: mobilizing people on the basis of the injustice of an act, defying the authority, going to jail, not resorting to violence even under provocation and keeping a hate-free relationship with the enemy.

For people to emerge as a moral force, they themselves should be transformed. He set up an ashram for like-minded people to live together. He ran journals to educate people on his ideas. Above all, he set an inspiring personal example. What he did in South Africa he repeated in India, but on a larger scale.

He evolved his methods of protest in South Africa in the absence of any alternative to his leadership or his methods. His success in South Africa helped him to be a leader in India.

Gandhi stuck to his methods despite grave provocations to the strategy – unleashing of violence by the British, or revenge acts by the Indians. Through his well-publicized movements, he exposed the moral bankruptcy of the British rule to the whole world. In the end his unique methods won freedom for India with least violence and ill-will towards the rulers. The non-violent methods he taught to the people in resisting authority helped India resolve conflicts politically and stay democratic.

His non-violent methods directed against communalism were not as successful. He could not stop the division of India along religious lines and the communal violence that came in its wake. However, at the peak of communal madness in Calcutta in 1947, through fasting he made the people of both communities stop violence.

But by speaking for Muslims, Gandhi antagonized some Hindus who thought Gandhi was responsible for the partition. Nathuram Godse, who shot Gandhi dead, was one among them.

When Mahatma was killed by a man of his own religion, India was stunned. That senseless act exposed the nature of communalism and the politics of hatred. Thus it laid foundations to secularism. Through life he taught peace and through death he taught peace.

Gandhi was inspired by the trial and death of Socrates and in the end made his own death an authentic statement of his philosophy.

Conservative elements

Gandhi is undoubtedly creative in many aspects, but very orthodox in certain matters. His defense of the caste system despite opposing untouchability is an example of this. His outdated views on caste and his forcing of Ambedkar to drop separate electorates antagonized many scheduled castes.

In spiritual aspects, he blindly followed the philosophy of self-control. He took the oath of celibacy at some stage during his life. And at 77, he wanted to see, by sleeping naked with young girls, if he could overcome the sexual desire! Like Ramakrishna Paramahamsa and others before him, Gandhi regarded freedom from lust as a part of self-cleansing. And such cleansing was supposed to enhance one's power of transforming the evil!

Even fasting was supposed to be an act of self-cleansing – no doubt, Ambedkar was entitled to a different opinion on the matter.

On the economic front, Gandhi did not understand the role of technology in producing wealth. Nor did he understand the power of division of labour in creating prosperous societies.

♦ ♦ ♦

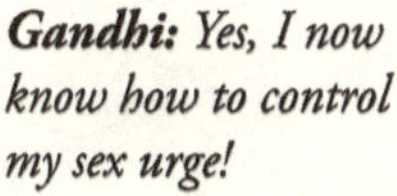

Questions to think about

1. What is 'Truth' according to Gandhi?
2. What are the conservative elements in Gandhism regarding
   - self-control
   - opposition to machinery
   - opposition to specialisation
   - defence of the caste system

23. Rabindranath Tagore

In two areas, Rabindranath Tagore (1861-1941) held very unusual ideas which are as important now as when they were expressed. The first area refers to his ideas of what education should be; the second refers to his opposition to the promotion of nationalism. These views have ethical implications.

(1) Education often is goal-oriented and future-driven. It involves going through a lot of pain for a certain result in the end. Tagore was against this. He said education should be such that a child should learn to enjoy the present in a deeper way. Dance, drama, music, painting and reading stories etc. are a part of the curriculum.

He wants the classroom to be close to nature. In his school at Santiniketan, West Bengal, students live close to nature – sitting under the trees, watching animals and plants, sensing seasonal changes, and having flexible schedules. And knowledge should be derived as directly as possible from the natural settings. "We rob the child of his earth to teach him geography, of language to teach him grammar."

Education should show how to celebrate life. It is not simply a means to earn one's livelihood. Nor is it only a means to earn wealth or power.

A child brought up as Tagore wants is of course a happier child and least likely to behave unethically.

Tagore: *A happy child-hood is the foundation of morality.*

(2)   Tagore differed from most of his contemporaries, including Gandhi, in holding nationalism as a narrow ideology. He took it to be an evil and held it responsible for the wars during his time. Tagore did not think – as Gandhi did – that nationalism can take man towards internationalism or universal brotherhood.

Tagore believed that education should promote understanding of people belonging to different nations, faiths, religions and cultures. It should bring down the barriers across cultures rather than strengthen them. It should promote sense of oneness, universal brotherhood.

This he taught when his fellow Indians were promoting nationalism to fight against colonialism.

Questions to think about

1. What are Tagore's views on education?
2. Discuss the differences between Gandhi and Tagore on the issue of nationalism.

24. Mother Teresa

Born in Skopje, Macedonia, in 1910, Mother Teresa joined the Sisters of Loreto in Dublin in 1928 and was sent to India. She taught at St. Mary's High School in Calcutta from 1931 to 1948, until leaving the Loreto order to set up the Missionaries of Charity. Through her sisters, brothers and priests her service to the poorest of the poor spread all over the world. She won many awards including the Nobel Peace Prize in 1979. After her death in 1997, the process for her sainthood was quickly begun and she was beatified in 2003.

***

What are the ethical implications of her work? At the time of Mother Teresa's death, the Missionaries of Charity had over 4000 sisters and an associated brotherhood of 300 members, operating 610 missions in 123 countries. This is an inspiring example of massive mobilization of people for altruistic work in the 20th century.

Her sisters and brothers seek no profits, take no salaries and lead a life of simplicity and religiousness. The people they serve are not just the poor, but the poorest of the poor – those who are abandoned, those who live, as per Mother Teresa, not in poverty but in misery: the dying, the diseased and the forsaken.

According to Mother Teresa, this service is voluntary – in fact, not just voluntary but that it should be done with love. She says, what matters is not what material things we give or to how many we give but how much we love them.

But why love? That is the way to do one's own work. One works only for Jesus. A hungry man is a hungry Jesus. A naked man is a naked Jesus. If the work is a burden, don't work. If it is being done out of pity, please stop it. If you want to earn a name from this, please don't use the premises of the Missionaries. Purity of heart and love for God are the only foundations for this work, she affirms.

People all over the world have contributed to her work. That her work moved so many people shows something about the human motivation system. It challenges traditional understanding of what motivates man.

Essentially, selfless work moves people. It challenges them to cooperate. Mother Teresa used this trait of man for social work. Mahatma Gandhi used this for political work. Both of them were mobilizing the nobler end within the spectrum of human motivation. Through selfless work, man discovers the nobler side of himself and feels happy.

***

Mother Teresa's work did not escape criticism. Some said that the inmates were not looked after well, medical care being inadequate. Some said that she served the poor without bothering to see how they could lead lives independently. Some alleged that she took money from people of dubious integrity and that she spent a big part of the money she received on religious activities and that she campaigned against abortion and family planning.

Such criticism would be valid if Mother Teresa had claimed that she was a perfect being or Goddess herself. She never made such claims. She was not a social scientist: she was not concerned with the economic and political factors that shaped the world. She did not reflect on what kind of economic and political systems generate this poverty. Nor did she try to find out who was exploiting whom. She took money from whoever gave it and gave it to whoever needed it. It was that simple for her. Was she right in accepting money from rogues? Why not? Taking money from them was a way of showering love on them.

Her ideas of religion are not a result of any rational understanding. Much discarded ideas of religion were sacred to her. So she advocated them.

We had better take her as one simple person, who knows only one thing – to love. She showed the power of love in human organization. A rational critic, a political rebel and a philosopher should take this lesson from her life and apply it in his/her own work to create a better society.

Mother Teresa never said her work was the highest kind of work, but only held that love – and not narrow obsession with oneself – is the noblest state of mind with which one should work.

A good mother doesn't tell her child, 'Do what I do,' but only, 'Do what you like. I am with you.'

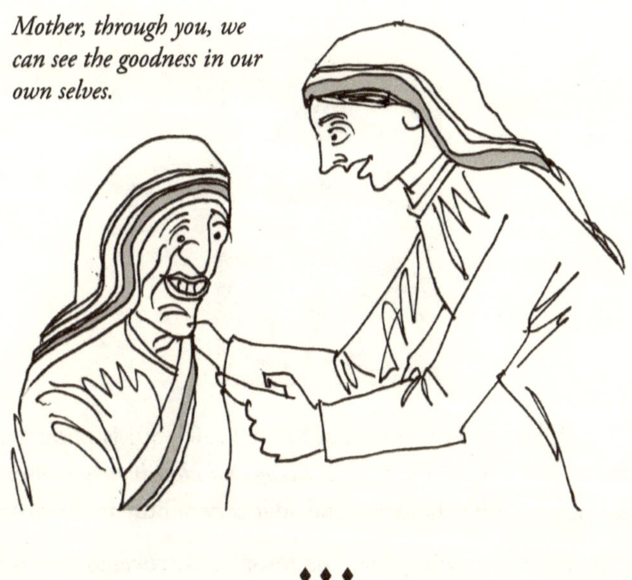

♦ ♦ ♦

Questions to think about

1. Discuss how Mother Teresa's work is related to her view of religion.

25. Jean-Paul Sartre

The philosophy of Jean-Paul Sartre (1905-80) is known as *existentialism*. His major work is *Being and Nothingness* (1943). He is known for his discovery and advocacy of human freedom.

One way of knowing how a philosopher discovered freedom is to know to what he had been bonded. Sartre had held the idea that each individual has essence in him – the essence of his true nature – and that individual should act upon the essence, and that God gave the essence.

Sartre's existentialism is based on phenomenology, which was started by Kant. But Sartre got more direct inspiration from Edmund Husserl and Martin Heidegger. *Being and Nothingness* was supposed to complement Heidegger's *Being and Time*. Phenomenology proposed that reality is constructed. Existentialism focused on how self is constructed.

Self is a matter of construct – individuals have an image of it, they keep altering it. It is neither fixed nor is it pre-determined. The Buddha and Ramana would say it is a construct and unreal and one need not have it – that is how Eastern tradition developed. But Sartre's conclusion is different.

156

That the individual has no essence and that there is no God providing any essence led Sartre to argue that man is "condemned to be free". By accepting that there is no God he is acting on Nietzsche's declaration that "God is dead."

Sartre felt free: 'no essence' meant freedom from the past; 'no God' meant no need to fear divine judgment and so freedom from the future. Thus Sartre stood for celebration of human freedom.

Human beings do not have any essence before their existence. There are no predetermined routes in life by which their essence is to be expressed. They come into the world with no preordained predispositions. "Existence precedes essence," declared Sartre.

He wrote first about individual freedom, then he moved on to freedom of societies – how people should fight against authority. He once embraced Marxism, but after seeing the abuses perpetrated in its name, he liked being labeled an anarchist!

***

That self is a construct is used to show the nature of conflict in relationships. One has an image of what one is. One has an image of what one is in the eyes of others. These images do not match. Understanding is sought but not given. Much of the conflict is in attempting to match these images.

In Sartre's play *No Exit*, a man and two women are kept in a room after their death. They were expecting a tormentor, who never came. They started conversing and got into conflict. They realized that no tormentor was supposed to come and 'hell is other people.'

The door was closed when the man wanted to run away. On one occasion, the door did open but the man didn't run away saying to the woman 'I am yet to convince you that I had not led a cowardly life!' It implies that one is constantly choosing hell to convince the other of the truth of one's self image!

Why does man want to reduce this gap? It is said that the image of oneself is not independently formed. It is influenced by what others think of oneself. So man wants to work out his own salvation through improving others' opinion of him. Precisely, such a process ties him to hell.

In Sartre's play *The Condemned of Altona*, the protagonist is responsible for the murder of many Jews.

Consciousness of this crime prevents him from having a decent image of himself. Unable to resume normal life even after many years he commits suicide. This can mean that construction of self can't be completely divorced from reality.

It means a construct is not unrelated to the real. One can't murder the innocent and yet have a nice self-image. This link between the image and the actual forces one to be good – hence this is a source of ethics.

♦♦♦

Questions to think about

1. What is meant by existentialism?
2. Is 'self' a construct? Explain.
3. How is R.D. Laing influenced by Sartre?

26. Psychology of emotions

Emotions and evolution

How do we react in ways that we are ourselves surprised? And should we be reacting more often that way?

Understanding the working of the brain explains such reactions. Suppose you suddenly see a snake near your bed, you will be terrified and run away. You are responding to the emotion of fear. You are likely to think that is an appropriate response.

But when you find yourself in a psychologically threatening situation and you run away from it, you may regret your reaction later. You may conclude that you should have faced the situation.

Or when you felt somebody was about to insult you and you might have said something only to regret it later. It means you responded to the threat inappropriately, unthinkingly.

We know now that the biological mechanisms that respond to the threat of a snake or insult are the same. Why is that so? That was how the brain evolved. It was first suited to face physical danger. The same system is working for a symbolic threat too.

What is the biological mechanism behind the actions that are not done with reflection? A visual signal goes from the *retina* to the *thalamus*, where it is translated into the language of the brain. Then visual messages go to the *visual cortex* where it is analyzed and assessed – these are called functions of the intellect. And then messages from the cortex go to *amygdala* for appropriate response. Then we feel our response is conscious and thought-out.

But research has found that this is not the only sequence. A smaller portion of the original data goes from thalamus to amygdala directly. And if the external stimulus is dangerous enough, emotional response is triggered which is not a result of reflection.

It means sensory data is acted upon without processing. This mechanism is adaptive if the situation really calls for immediate response. But this is maladaptive if the response badly requires reflection.

Daniel Goleman says this is a case of *emotional hijacking* – instantaneous acting of emotions without reflecting upon the consequences.

Studies by Benjamin Libet

Benjamin Libet (1916-2007) developed procedures to study decision-making processes in the brain. Each participant would be asked to perform a simple motor action like pressing a particular button. Electroencephalogram (EEG) electrodes would be affixed to the scalp to study brain activity. In one experiment, there was a gap of 200 milliseconds between conscious decision and the action. But the brain activity associated with the action started around 500 milliseconds before. So through the study of brain activity, researchers could predict which button would be pressed – even before the subject himself knew.

This study shows there are different decision-making systems in the brain – one at the unconscious level and another at the rational and conscious level. In some cases unconscious-level decisions are acted upon and in some other cases they are vetoed.

What factors influence decisions at the unconscious level? The consequences of previous decisions do influence. Pavlovian impulses play an important role at the unconscious level.

Biological terms

1. *Thalamus*: This is located just above the *midbrain*. It consists of two egg-shaped groups of nerve cell nuclei. It acts as a sensory relay station, directing incoming information from the sense receptors (such as vision, hearing) to the cerebrum.

   The *midbrain* is located in the middle of the brain. The *hindbrain* includes all the structures located in the hind (posterior) part of the brain, closest to the spinal cord. The *forebrain* includes the structures located in the front (anterior) part of the brain.

2. *Brainstem*: This is also called *central core*. This controls involuntary behavior such as coughing, sneezing and primitive behavior under voluntary control such

as breathing, vomiting, sleeping, eating, drinking, temperature regulation and sexual behavior. This is at the centre if the brain is thought of in terms of three concentric layers. The next layer is the *limbic system*, which controls our emotions. Above that is the *cerebrum* which regulates our higher intellectual processes.

3. *Limbic system:* This is a set of structures that impose additional control over some of the instinctive behaviors regulated by the central core. Fish and reptiles have rudimentary limbic systems. They carry out activities such as feeding, attacking, fleeing and mating by means of stereotyped behavior. In mammals, the limbic system seems to inhibit some of these instinctive patterns and allow the organism to be more flexible and better able to adapt to changes in the environment.

4. *The amygdala* is an almond-shaped structure in the limbic system. This is critical to emotions such as fear. Monkeys with damage to amygdala exhibit marked reduction in fear. Humans with such damage are unable to recognize facial expressions of fear.

5. *Neuron:* This is the basic unit of the *nervous system*. This is a specialized cell that transmits neural impulses or messages to other neurons, glands and muscles. There are many types of neurons.   But all have common structures. Projecting from the *cell body* or *soma* are a number of short branches called *dendrites*, which receive neural impulses from other neurons. The *axon* is a slender tube that extends from the soma and transmits these messages to other neurons. At its end, the axon

is divided into a number of branches called *synaptic terminals* or *terminal buttons*.

The *nervous system* includes the central nervous system (brain and spinal cord) and peripheral nervous system (somatic system and autonomic system).

6. *Homo sapiens sapiens* are the modern humans who first appeared only 50,000 years ago. Modern humans have an average brain size of 1300 cc. Homo erectus had an average cranial capacity of 1000 cc. Homo erectus may have first appeared around 1.8 million years ago. The *Australopithecus africanus* had an average cranial capacity of only 440 cc – not much larger than that of chimpanzees. It lived around 3 million years ago. [Around 500 million years ago, our ancestors were in the form of fish in a primitive form. From fish the amphibians evolved. Then reptiles, out of which the mammals evolved.

7. *Pavlovian conditioning* is also called *classical conditioning*. It is a learning process in which a previously neutral stimulus becomes associated with another stimulus through repeated pairing with the stimulus. When the sound of a bell is repeatedly associated with food, dog salivates when it hears the bell, Pavlov demonstrated.

Emotions in decision-making

There is a popular view that good decisions are rational decisions and they are emotion-free. This view stands disproved by elaborate research that shows decisions can't be made without reference to emotions. Research by Antonio Damasio, a neurologist, on decision-making is very significant in this context.

The results of his study become intelligible if one sees them in the context of evolution. Decision-making had been going on even in the simplest life forms that did not have brains. Involvement of the brain in decision-making is a later development. Complex decisions – be it regarding movement, feeding, fighting, responding to threat – are taken on the basis of emotions.

What do we mean by emotions? Maybe we can take them as plus/minus states. Body harm is minus, food is a plus. When the organism senses harm, it takes certain decisions. When it senses food, it takes certain decisions. Life forms from the beginning have been surviving by good decision-making. So decision-making didn't start with the humans. Nor did it start with the brain.

As advanced forms of life evolved, the brain was not designed afresh. Something new was put over the old. So the old systems continued but with the additional mechanisms for advanced functioning. Cortex was added for advanced processing. What is added is good for processing. But research shows that by itself it can't decide. Decision-making involves amygdala and its related circuits. If the links between emotional circuits and cortex activity are snapped, decision-making is paralyzed.

Elliot was a successful lawyer before the tumor behind his forehead was removed. After the surgery which was considered successful he could not keep his job. His wife left him. He wasted his savings. It was then that he approached Damasio to know if something was wrong with him neurologically. At first Damasio couldn't find anything wrong – his intellectual abilities

were intact. But when Damasio asked Elliot when they could meet again, Elliot explained, dispassionately, plus and minus of many days for the next meeting but was not in a position to decide which day he could meet! From that instance Damasio hypothesized that something done to him during the surgery had impaired his decision-making capacity. Damasio found that the prefrontal-amygdala circuit – which links emotion with reasoning – was damaged, leading to lots of analyses but no decision.

Damasio then designed tests to probe the role of emotions in decisions. In what is called *the gambling task,* subjects are asked to pick up cards – A, B, C and D. Each card carries a reward but on occasion some penalty. Rewards and penalties are arranged in such a way that if A and B are picked up often, the subjects will end up gaining. If C and D are picked up often, the subjects will end up losing. A and B carry higher rewards but lower penalties. The subjects are supposed to make this out for themselves. They do not even know when the game will end. It is found that those with impaired brains could not move towards A and B. Among the normal, some moved towards A and B faster than others. Among the better-performing subjects, a higher level of activity is seen in that prefrontal region which in Elliot's case was damaged.

Damasio explained the outcome in terms of *somatic marker hypothesis.* He said that memory traces of consequences of decisions are formed in ventromedial prefrontal cortex (vmPFC) – recording of plus and minus of our decisions. Successful recording leads to effective decision-making. Emotions are thus a part of decision-making.

But let us not forget that plus and minus in advanced organisms are symbolic. What is a plus and what is a minus is determined by rational processes. Much romantic literature has been written glorifying the emotional, which is only apparently reason-free. The literature unduly considers the primitive (call it the fish in man, since man came from fish) truly authentic. It does not consider that the fish, the primitive, only acts swimming in the ocean of reason, the evolved part.

Empathy and biology

Leslie Brothers, a psychiatrist, conducted experiments on primates to study empathy. Two monkeys are made to fear a tone that has been associated with an electric shock. Later the monkeys are made to learn to press a lever to avoid the shock. They are then put in separate cages connected through a closed circuit TV through which they can see each other's face. When one monkey hears the tone, the other one, though not hearing the tone but seeing the distressed face of the other, presses the lever. This is an act of empathy.

When wild monkeys are brought to the lab and the connections between the cortex and the amygdala are severed, it is found after their release from the lab that they have a difficult time relating emotionally with others. Though they can do things like climbing and feeding themselves, they eventually live as isolates.

The study shows that empathy is inherited and if its biological basis is damaged, empathy will be affected.

What are its implications for morality? We know that the roots of morality are in empathy. We also know psychopaths are those who have lost this ability of empathy somewhere.

Robert Levenson, a psychologist, studied the nature of empathy among people. When two people are in empathy, one's own physiology tracks the other. It goes through the same emotions.

Levenson says there are three dimensions to empathy: seeing other's pain, feeling it, healing it. One may see/understand the other, but may not feel it. Or one may feel the distress of the other but may not be able to heal or may be unwilling to heal.

If we understand that morality enables managing complex organizations, empathy may have been placed at the higher end of evolution.

Suppose the earth is slowly flooded with water and a new kind of fish evolves from humans, this new fish will be different from the old primitive fish.

Attunement

Daniel Stern, a psychiatrist, studied relationship between children and their mothers. In a case of twin boys, their mother perceived that one son to be like her and was well-attuned to that boy but not so with the other boy. This difference was first observed when the boys were just three months old. With her favored boy, she would gaze only when the boy wanted and avoid gaze when he didn't want. However, with the other boy, she would impose a gaze and make him uncomfortable. A year later, the mis-attuned child was found to be more fearful and dependent than the well-attuned. Stern says mis-attunement takes emotional toll on the child and he will have difficulty in empathizing.

Three-month-old babies of depressed mothers mirrored their mothers' moods displaying more anger and sadness.

A study of criminals showed that those who had committed most violent crimes didn't have opportunity for healthy attunement in their childhood.

Emotional Intelligence

Daniel Goleman through his 1995 book *Emotional Intelligence* popularized the term *emotional intelligence* (EI). His book was based on the work done by psychologists such as Peter Salovey and John Mayer, who suggest that there are four critical components of EI.

The first component is accurate perception and expression of emotions. One should be able to read distress or happiness or other emotions in others as well as in oneself. One should be able to read them in voices, gestures and works of art. Empathy is difficult without this. Also one should be able to communicate one's emotions.

The second component is the ability to access and generate emotions in the service of thinking and problem-solving. Emotions provide the basis for decision-making, reasoning and creativity.

The third component is the ability to understand emotional meanings. We may know we are anxious but we also need to know why we are anxious. Attributing the emotion to the relevant source is important. One should be able to analyze the antecedent events as well as the outcomes of emotional experiences.

The final component is emotional regulation. This refers to the ability to manage and regulate emotions appropriately. Letting emotions rage unabated is unhealthy. Equally unhealthy is controlling them completely.

Emotional Intelligence can be learnt. Recognizing feelings and managing them can be a part of education, training or psychotherapy.

Can EI be measured?

Salovey and Mayer expressed the view that some people possess greater ability than others to reason about and use emotion-laden information to improve both their cognitive ability and social functioning.

The four-branch model of EI consists of perceiving emotions, using them, understanding them and managing them. These abilities can be measured by performance tests.

Mayer-Salovey-Caruso EI Test (MSCEIT) is designed to assess these four branches of EI. Individuals with higher MSCEIT scores report better quality relationships. Higher scores for married people report more satisfaction and less conflict in marriage.

College students with higher scores report lower levels of drug and alcohol consumption and fewer deviant acts including stealing, gambling and fighting. This shows the link between EI and ethics.

Higher scores represent decreased levels of anxiety and depression.

EI is associated with a number of important outcomes in the workplace. Those with higher scores are rated effective in handling stress and creating a congenial working environment.

So the concept of EI has important implications at home, school and workplace.

However, there is no consensus on measuring EI. MSCEIT comes under the ability model of EI, which takes EI as a distinct ability. Some prefer to take EI as part of a set of personality dispositions. That type of measurement is called the mixed or trait model of EI.

Marshmallow test

This test is done to study the level of impulse control in kids. A four-year-old is told either to eat one marshmallow (soft, white sweet) now or two marshmallows after 15 minutes. Walter Mischel during the 1960s conducted this test on the children of faculty and the staff of Stanford. The same children were tracked 14 years later. The difference between those who waited for the second marshmallow and those who didn't was huge. Those who could delay gratification when they were children turned out to be more self-reliant, confident and dependable. More surprisingly, they had dramatically higher SAT scores compared to the others.

It shows there are differences at a very early age in gratification-delaying ability. This ability is important in managing emotions. It turns out that this is important for academic excellence as well. Enhancing this ability should be a part of good parenting.

♦ ♦ ♦

Questions to think about

1. What do you know about thalamus, amygdala, stem brain, cortex?

2. Explain the basics of evolution as per Darwin.

3. What is conditioning?

4. What is somatic marker hypothesis?

5. What is emotional hijacking?

6. What do you know about the following?
   - The importance of emotional intelligence (EI)
   - The components of EI
   - Ways of measuring EI
   - Studies on empathy, attunement, emotional regulation

7. Why are some people more effective in employing emotions in decision-making?

8. Discuss the implications of Damasio's studies on the role of emotions in decision-making.

27. R.D. Laing

Indian philosophers inquired for centuries the process of self-dissolution, which is called nirvana or moksha. This is held as the highest spiritual pursuit of man. This ideal gives the impression, quite wrongly, that self is primarily a negative thing.

Indian philosophers never went into exploring the positive value of self. They don't know how self can be mutilated and how mutilated self can wreak havoc on the life of the individual.

We understand the problems of mutilation of self when we try to understand the individuals who are regarded as clinically insane. Philosophers never paid attention to such individuals. Neither J Krishnamurti nor Ramana ever tried to bring back the 'crazy' or 'insane' to normal. They only tried to reveal to the normal some beyond-self and beyond-normal processes of awareness.

We can say they completely ignored the underworld of self, which is the specialization of psychiatrists. One such specialist on this underworld is R.D. Laing (1927-89). The study of the underworld of self is important for the purpose of comprehensive understanding of self. Indian philosophy's

174

bashing of self prevents comprehensive understanding of self. Laing provides a much-needed corrective.

***

A math student learns math by solving problems. He uses the trial-and-error method. First he approaches a problem in a particular way. If he gets the answer he becomes assured of his understanding. If he does not, he will realize that something is missing in his understanding. When he learns the solution, his understanding of the math improves. He can't learn math without solving problems. By feeling good when he solves and feeling bad when he fails, he learns the subject of math.

Similar is man's orientation to the psychological world. He seeks others' support and help. He seeks their respect and love. These are the psychological rewards he is after. He responds to a situation in a particular way to get the reward. When he does not get the reward, he alters his behavior. If he succeeds in getting the reward, then he learns how to behave.

Initial responses of a child are authentic – he responds with his true feelings. When he learns that responding with his true feelings is very risky and unrewarding, he begins to hide his true feelings and may choose to pretend.

Pretending occasionally with people less important in life may not damage true self – let us call it s_t. But if one has to pretend often and with people very important in life – family members, for example – then under certain circumstances a false self – let us call it s_f – can be created in the individual. The child may learn to deal with the world with s_f with most people, most of the time.

How will this affect working of the true self? Since it is not being expressed, it will not get the feedback from the environment. It will not learn. It will not grow. In effect, it will be impoverished. This impoverishment will only contribute to strengthening of the false self. As s_f gets more involved, s_t becomes poorer.

What is wrong if a person works with s_f instead of s_t – as long as he is getting along well? He is not getting along well. He does experience a sense of not-me. He perceives the situation to be not-real. As he loses his authenticity, the world around him loses its authenticity – everything appears unreal. He can neither trust anyone nor feel trusted by anyone. He can neither give love nor receive it. Out of touch with himself, he is out of touch with the external.

Moreover, maintaining a false-self requires a lot of effort – lot of hiding, lot of false things. This is a tiresome process. One easily gets exhausted. One can't enjoy the company of others. One wants to avoid others – for fear of being found out.

So false-self can't really solve the problems that true-self fails to solve. Instead, it creates a new set of problems.

***

Impoverished true-self and active false-self prepare the ground for a variety of abnormal outcomes. One may complain, 'I observe my body as if I am external to the body. I am not in my body, but outside of it.' This means mind-body split is taking place. Self is running out of the body: self is becoming, as Laing calls, *un-embodied*. This is a source of great anxiety to the individual.

At one stage, s_t is aware of s_f. At a more advanced stage, s_f can completely occupy the body, and s_t may know nothing about it. Or an individual may learn to create multiple false selves – s_{f1}, s_{f2}, s_{f3} – to face diverse situations. They may occupy the body one at a time – just as individuals log into a particular computer one at a time. Or s_{f1} may notice s_{f2} or s_{f3} as it is logging in and the other logging out of the body.

One is no longer *one* – no longer an individual, an undivided entity. One becomes *divided self*, as Laing calls it. It is all a mess. The way out is to fuse the divided selves into one – to get back to authenticity, slowly, step by step.

***

Psychiatry is a strange field. Often the aggressors bring their victims to the psychiatrists, when the aggressors are unsatisfied with the outcome of their aggression. Laing found the family to be playing an extremely important role in creating this kind of psychological chaos. In the name of love, he said, enormous violence is inflicted on the children. A considerable part of insanity is rooted in the child's inability to face the aggression unleashed from close quarters.

***

What are the ethical implications of all this? Ethical behavior requires, first of all, a healthy self – a self that is integrated. The chaos inside disrupts the normal process of learning, normal process of empathy or internalization of morality. Most abnormal crimes are committed by people who are chaotic inside.

Socrates may say, 'virtue is knowledge,' but such knowledge is impossible for a divided-self to attain. He may say, 'unexamined life is not worth living', but a divided-self will not have the capacity to examine. It stands crippled. It demands extra care.

Laing: Jesus, if your father is kind,
He will close down hell and open
a rehabilitation centre in heaven
for sinners.

♦ ♦ ♦

Questions to think about

1. What is meant by divided self?

2. How will divided self impact emotional intelligence?

3. What is the implication of Laing's theory for parenting?

28. Patricia Churchland

If 'A' is concerned about 'B', is 'A' feeling as per his biology? Or is it that biologically 'A' should be concerned only about himself, and if 'A' is showing concern for 'B' is it only due to socialization?

Put differently, can biology explain concern for others? Or does biology rule out such a thing? Can it explain altruism – helping behavior, even risking one's comforts for the sake of others? The work of Patricia Churchland provides answers.

Before discussing her work, we can review certain debates on Darwinism. The essence of Darwinism was taken to be the 'survival of the fittest'. But what constitutes 'better fit'? It was usually thought to be the ability to fight for one's food, for oneself. 'Better fit' meant having more energy, a stronger will to fight – in other words, more aggression. Better fit did not mean helping others, having feelings for others.

So, many biologists concluded that aggression, like sex, is biologically inherited and helping behavior is not, but wondered why so many animals showed a pronounced helping behavior. To them aggression seemed in sync with natural selection and

180

altruism didn't. Churchland's work should be read in that context.

Patricia Churchland showed that like aggression and sex, altruism too is inherited. Species vary in terms of the level of altruism that is inherited. At higher levels of evolution, altruism is introduced.

Organisms at a lower level of evolution have the attitude of '*me*' and 'me alone'. They do not have a helping behavior. But at a higher level, organisms will have concern for not just *me*, but *mine* too. It means an organism will have caring attitude not simply towards itself but towards its offspring as well. Self-care is extended to kin-care. With the evolution of mammals, this concern for *mine* is pronounced. Mothers nurture their offspring – taking care of them, even risking their own lives to protect their offspring.

First it is 'me.' Next, it is 'me + mine'. Next, kith too included. As pre-frontal structures expand, extensions of this kind take place. Man is concerned about himself, his offspring and even his group. This is all part of biology. So it is not true that self-concern is biologically inherited and concern for others is socially induced. Concern for others has a biological basis.

Altruism is not against the spirit of evolution. Evolution would not have happened the way it did if altruism had not been passed on biologically.

When organism is moving from *me* to *me+ kin*, next to *me+ kin+ kith*, its ability to trust others is increasing. Patricia found that the level of trust is linked to a particular peptide – called *oxytocin*. This is not the only peptide but it is an important one. Among the Prairie Voles, the female cares for the offspring and its mate too takes care of the pups. However, among Montane

Voles, which are very similar to Prairie Voles, the female cares for the offspring but its mate has nothing to do with taking care of the pups. Among Prairie Voles, there is mate attachment. But among the Montane Voles, there is no mate attachment. Why is this differrence? Prairie Voles have more of oxytocin and vasopressin, its equivalent! Higher levels of oxytocin required certain changes in the structure of the brain. In the experiments it is shown that by blocking oxytocin among the Prairie Voles, mate attachment can be crippled!

A mother feels happy when its offspring is around and happy, feels distressed when the offspring is away and unsafe. The pain of her offspring is as bad as the pain to herself. Pleasure of her offspring is as good as pleasure to herself.

Organisms have been wired so. These are the differences in endocrinology across the species – which made nursing and parenting possible. This kin-care is consistent with natural selection. The history of evolution of mammals is nothing but the history of evolution of the family.

As organisms evolved, sociability or sociality evolved. Without this, hugely complex social systems would not have been possible. Expansion in pre-frontal structures reinforced the extension of the pleasure-pain system from oneself to others related to self in a variety of ways.

♦ ♦ ♦

Questions to think about

1. Is altruism anti-biological?

2. Is kindness anti-biological?

3. What is the role of altruism in evolution?

4. What peptide is involved in nurturing behaviour?

5. What is the difference between Prairie Voles and Montane Voles in terms of kin behaviour? How is the difference explained?

6. Does Patricia Churchland successfully counter Nietzsche's reading of Darwinism?

29. Antonio Damasio

Damasio's *Self Comes to Mind* (2010) brings out the most recent research done in the field of neuroscience on the issues of mind, self and consciousness. This book has huge implications for Indian philosophy which makes very radical propositions in terms of self and consciousness.

This book does not explicitly address Indian philosophy. But it explains many processes of the human mind so clearly that it can legitimately be considered to be a milestone in the evolution of philosophy – Indian one in particular.

Brain and mind

The question 'Where is the brain?' is not difficult to answer. It is inside the skull. It can be touched and photographed. One important aspect of human evolution is the increase in the brain size. We have data regarding the average size of the brain as evolution progressed. It is a physical thing.

The question 'What is the mind?' has never been that easy to answer. It can't be touched, nor can it be photographed. One can't see what is in others' minds.

The mind is something that emerges out of the brain. To know how the mind can emerge out of the brain, we must know what the brain does. The brain is made up of neurons, the cells that communicate through the flow of electric charge. The brain is connected to the body proper – Damasio takes the body minus the brain as *body proper* – through the network of neurons. The brain controls and commands the body proper. How does it do it?

The brain draws *neural maps* (like photos) of the body proper, and also of itself. When a body part is hurt, the map changes. Some intervention takes place to restore the balance. If a foot is hurt, the cause of the hurt can be removed through intervention. So neural maps help in body regulation – be it temperature regulation, blood flow or some other function.

Think of a shopping mall with cc cameras and a control room. Through the cameras one can watch what is going on in a remote corner of the mall. If anyone is found stealing, he can be caught. The brain is that cameras and images. But with one difference. In the shopping mall, management watches through the cameras and intervenes on that basis. In the case of the brain, the intervention is automatic – there is no one managing the brain.

There is one more difference. In the mall, a cc camera can only take images of the mall. It can't create images on its own. If a theft is taking place, it can't have normal images. If everything is normal, it can't create the image of a theft. It is a passive recorder of the mall. On the other hand, the brain creates *as-if images* (my words please, not Damasio's). What is the purpose of these as-if images? Through them, the brain arrives at the required solution.

So that is the link between the brain and the body proper. Through actual as well as as-if images the brain monitors and regulates the body proper.

Damasio surprises us by proposing that whatever goes on between the brain and the outer world is similar to what goes on between the brain and the body proper. How does the brain map the outer world? Through the sensory organs – eyes, ears, nose, mouth, and skin. A square is stored differently from a circle; a song is distinguished from traffic noise. So in a nutshell, what are the senses? These are the outposts of the brain. The brain makes actual as well as as-if images of the outer world.

Given that this is what the brain does, how is the mind defined? The mind is the flow of images. These images are based on neural maps – neural maps are of the brain and images of the mind. By image, we mean all types of sensory images, not just the visual ones.

What is the mind? Partly, it is what thoughts are. What are thoughts? A thought is a flow of images – actual as well as as-if – of the past and of the future.

Thoughts are only a part of the mind. For example, the brain is making images of blood flow to the heart, which are not our thoughts. The mind is a flow of images – of the body proper and of the world. We can be conscious of the images of the outer world, but never of the body proper. So thoughts constitute only a part of the mind.

Can the mind exist without the brain? Damasio says, 'No.' To him, the mind can't come into existence without the brain. The mind, as a matter of definition, is nothing but the activity of the brain.

No self, no consciousness

What is self? It is this sense of 'I'. Do we always have this sense? Of course not. And certainly not when we are asleep.

What is consciousness? In other words, what is meant by being unconscious? When are we unconscious? In deep sleep, we lose consciousness. If a person is in coma, he has no consciousness. If anaesthesia is given, a person loses consciousness temporarily.

In a deep sleep, we lose consciousness completely. But when we are about to wake up, we tend to be somewhat conscious. So consciousness can be thought of in terms of a range – from 0 to 1 – from deep sleep to wakefulness.

When one is unconscious, what is it that one is not conscious of? One does not take any sensory data during deep sleep. So no data of the external. Does one have data about self? No. To be unconscious means blocking of all data.

What is one conscious of when one is fully awake? One is conscious of self as well as sensory data. A normal man is conscious of data from five senses. A blind man is conscious of data from only four senses. A blind and deaf person only from three senses. Extended, even if all the five senses are paralyzed, one can feel conscious as long as one has sense of self. In sum, the essence of consciousness is the presence of sense of self.

Consciousness emerged during a particular stage in the evolution. The brain had been doing the mapping and regulating the body. It had also been handling the external world. All this was being done nonconsciously. Somewhere along the line, self came to mind and thus consciousness was born.

During deep sleep, the brain has minimal activity, minimal mapping, and so minimal mind. During a dream, brain activity increases; more mapping is done; there is more mind. But self is not there. So that is a state of mind without self; there is no consciousness. Once you wake up, the brain resumes its activities, you call them thoughts. You know that you are there. In other words, you have become conscious.

Some people have *lucid dreams* – dreams in which they know they are dreaming. Trained lucid dreamers introduce a bit of self in their dream without disturbing the dream. Too much self, they will wake up. Too little, they will fall into proper dream. By introducing a bit of self, they become conscious enough to intervene in their dreams: they can choose to ride a tiger instead of running away from it.

Why did self come to mind?

Consciousness is the process of self entering the mind. Why did that happen? What are the advantages? Enormous. A body can survive longer if it manoeuvres itself within a certain range of behavior. A body used to sedentary work can't suddenly do manual labour, nor can one used to manual labour do academic work. To operate within a range, the body has to follow a pattern, ruling out extremes. Self can do this function in an efficient way. When a mind picks up self, the body gets the direction. A bus with one steering wheel and a driver can cover a long distance. What a driver is to the vehicle, self is to the body.

Where is the self? Though self is spread over different parts of the brain, damage to a particular side of the brainstem can chuck out self. Damage to that part is what takes a man into coma. Damage to another part of the brainstem retains self but leads to the paralysis of the body. It is that specific.

That self is sourced in the brainstem, which is an ancient part of the brain, means that self had emerged long before the humans. So self/ consciousness is not unique to humans.

Damasio divides self into three levels – *protoself, coreself, autobiographical self.* Simpler life forms have simpler selves. Their selves are not as elaborate as ours. Humans have complex autobiographical selves – in which a lot of data of their past, present and future missions is stored. Autobiographical self is a memory bank.

So a human self is not simply a sense of me. It has big memory, with many folders and files. All this can be called *contents of consciousness,* which are the same as *contents of self.*

Lower levels of self perform certain core functions, such as, knowing where one's body is or where one's body ends. For a human being, to be awake is to have all the levels of self. For example, when you are suddenly woken up from a deep sleep, 'you' come to exist but you may take some time to figure out where you are. You experience this because in this instance all the levels of self are not booted simultaneously.

Emotions are not feelings

We normally do not make a distinction between emotions and feelings. Ordinarily they are used interchangeably. But Damasio makes a distinction, which does turn out to be crucial.

Feelings came along with consciousness – that is, with self. *You feel* pain. *You feel* pleasure. *You* should be there to *feel.* And those feelings are adaptive. You use feelings as a guide to behavior – trying to maximize pleasure and minimize pain. What guided an organism before feelings arrived, that is, before self emerged?

It was guided by *emotions.* Something negative is registered when the body is hurt. Something positive is registered when food is tasty. The brain steers the body through the memory of the positive and the negative. That is, through the emotions.

Do emotions disappear with the emergence of self? In other words, do we have emotions? Very much, we have emotions as well as feelings. Most of the work in the body is done through emotions – that is at a nonconscious level. Some work is done through feelings – that is, at a conscious level.

A slight decline in the flow of blood to the heart will leave a negative emotion and the brain intervenes without *you* knowing it. A huge part of work is thus done nonconsciously – with emotions. But decline below a certain level may give you pain that you will *feel* and will do something about it. A part of the work is thus done consciously – with feelings.

So positive and negative outcomes entering consciousness are feelings and those not entering are emotions. Many experiments show that emotions occur first and then we *feel and think* about what to do. When we see a snake, the body responds first through emotions: it is frightened. We may *feel* and *think* about it and discover that it is not a snake but a rope and *decide* not to run!

If an outsider can read your emotions, can he predict your responses before you make decisions? Studies show that a researcher monitoring your emotions through an equipment can predict your behavior before you *decide* what to do. It gives the impression that you are confirming what has already been nonconsciously decided on the basis of the emotions. Of course emotions may suggest a particular course of action and you may choose not to follow it. In such cases, the researcher can't predict your behavior before you decide.

Should we go by reason or feeling?

What is the role of reason in guiding behavior? Are we not rational beings? Emotions/feelings give a particular predisposition to act but reasoning can veto. You *feel* like slapping another person. But you will *reason* the consequences and so keep quiet. So we are emotive beings as well as rational beings.

Can we be free of emotions/feelings and become fully rational? Many thinkers had debated on this issue. Now neuroscience has many insights to offer on this issue. It says that we do an enormous amount of body-related work with the help of emotions and non-consciously. So we simply can't survive without emotions.

Even in conscious work, like decision-making, emotions play a crucial role. When there is a problem, there are many possible lines of actions. Emotions eliminate many possible lines and leave a few to be subjected to rational scrutiny. Even the final choice is made with the help of emotions. Decision-making is hugely impaired if we do not employ emotions in the process. In fact, the ability to employ emotions in the service of decision-making is a component of Emotional Intelligence.

From the conscious to the nonconscious

While some glorify reason unduly, some others glorify feeling unduly. To them, feeling is authentic whereas reasoning is inauthentic. Are they right? You may feel first and reason out afterwards. Dishonest reasoning, no doubt, is easier than dishonest feelings. But it doesn't necessarily follow that we should trust our feelings and not reasons. Why is it so?

Feelings are not independent of reasons. What you feel now may be the result of your earlier reasoning. If you reasoned that income is unjustly divided in the world, you may *feel* sorry for the less privileged. If you reasoned that poverty is due to laziness, you will *feel* contempt for the poor. So feelings are not independent of reasons; they can be the outcome of reasoning. The nonconscious banks on the conclusions of the conscious. The automated takes the outcomes of the deliberated.

The link between thinking/reasoning and feeling is evident in certain skills. When you are learning driving, you will be *thinking* about what to press to accelerate and what to press to apply the brakes. Through *thinking* you learn. What is learnt becomes part of your nonconscious responses. If you still need to *think* where the brake is and where the accelerator is, you should not take to the road. You are still a learner if you can't apply the brakes nonconsciously.

Musicians and sportspeople report they do not *think* while giving of their best. The hours and hours of practice pushed their skill into the nonconscious, that is, beyond the requirement of reasoning and thinking.

Conditioning

We can now examine what is meant by *conditioning*. It can be defined as an object or an event acquiring *emotional salience*. Say, an object to begin with did not stimulate any emotion. We call it an emotionally neutral object. Suppose an organism got hurt when it interacted with the object, then the object would come to be associated with a negative emotion. The organism will avoid the object next time. *Conditioning* is thus a process by which neutral objects/events acquire emotional salience.

Where is the data about positive and negative outcomes stored? In the brain – we call it memory. So memory contains neutral as well as charged images of the objects/events.

Why is the mind full of thoughts?

Now let us review our understanding of the mind. We said the mind is a flow of images. What are those images? They are based on neural maps – physical impressions created on the neurons – charged with emotions, that is, plus and minus outcomes.

We said the brain is a production house of as-if images. What are those as-if images? They are but desires and fears related to self.

A positive as-if image gives pleasure. A negative as-if image gives pain. A fantasy is profusion of pleasant as-if images. If the images are unpleasant, we call it a nightmare.

The brain is a busy production house. Why should the brain be producing the images all the time? Why is it busy producing as-if images even when it is not required to solve a problem?

Let us return to the analogy of the shopping mall. By fixing a nice image in the cc camera you can't change the mall. But the brain is different: an image in itself is the source of pleasure/pain and it can partially change the body. A sex fantasy, for example, is pleasurable in itself and it even leads to strong changes in the body!

Unlike the cc camera in the mall, the brain is creating a new level of reality through the as-if production. It is apparently addicted to this.

This explains why desires lead to thoughts, why the mind is full of thoughts, and why realization of a thoughtless state – the dream of religious seekers – is nearly impossible!

Not all thinking is reasoning

Though Damasio does not proceed this way, we can say, on closer examination, that thinking and reasoning are not one. 'If A leads to B, and B leads to C, then A leads to C' is an example of logical reasoning. What often goes on in the brain is not this kind of reasoning.

What goes on is a profusion of as-if images. And when a particular sequence of as-if images turns out to be more pleasant than others, we fix on it and make a decision to realize that image. So we decide not on the basis of logical reasoning but through a selection of as-if images. It means a lot of decision-making is done using feelings.

Future is past-bound

What is an as-if image? Any as-if image is a combination of the actual images. When we think of future, it is all various combinations of the present and the past. The future we desire is not totally new. In this way the future is past-bound. This appears to be an inherent limitation in the working of the brain.

Dysfunctions of self

The systems that evolved to defend the body are being used to defend self – more accurately, the autobiographical self rather than the protoself or the coreself. The autobiographical self is the record of personal data about the past, present and future plans. It may want to get more power, more respect, or more love.

The goals of the autobiographical self may sometimes increase risk to the body – as in many acts of revenge or a suicide. This means that the autobiographical self may fail to increase safety and security to a human being.

The sense of taste is evolved to distinguish the poisonous from the non-poisonous – to protect the body. But overeating for the sake of taste harms the body. In other words, what is functional at one level can be dysfunctional at another level.

There is need for more deliberate intervention in the working of the autobiographical self – to truly enhance the wellbeing of the organism. This is not something that Damasio talks about, but his work gives us greater clarity in proceeding with the transformation of self.

. . .

Krishnamurti: *During those long walks, not a single thought would pass my mind.*

Questions to think about

1. What do you know about the following?
   * The distinction between brain and mind
   * Uniqueness of neurons
   * Neural maps and images
   * Actual images, as-if images
   * Coma, anaesthesia, deep sleep
   * Self and consciousness
   * Reasons for self
   * Lucid dreams
   * Protoself, coreself, autobiographical self
   * Contents of self
   * Emotions and feelings
   * Reason and feeling
   * Reasoning and thinking
   * Conditioning

30. Sheldrake: Mind outside brain

Is consciousness in the world connected? Is there life after death? Is there a possibility of rebirth? How does karma work? Traditionally, science does not consider these questions as fit for investigation. But Dr. Rupert Sheldrake, a biologist, in his *Science Set Free* (2012) provides an interesting way to look at very diverse phenomena with a minimum set of propositions. His theory may be right or wrong, but it gives us a parsimonious way of looking at the diverse range of phenomena that occupy philosophy and religion. That is why it deserves consideration of sceptical minds.

Let us suppose the earth is currently populated by two species, A and B, with each species having around 10 members. A (2014, 1), A (2014, 2), A (2014, 3)… A (2014, 10) are members of A. Similarly members of B include B (2014, 1), B (2014, 2), B (2014, 3)… B (2014, 10). Traditionally, science considers the mind to be confining to the brain. Sheldrake's proposal is that the mind is a field based on a brain. So the mind is not confined to the skull.

What is a field? As Faraday defined, it is space modified.

Energy is stored through fields, and matter is an aspect of energy. This is to say that matter and fields are all connected.

The proposal that the mind is not confined to the brain also leads to the idea that memory is not confined to the brain! Like the data we input is not confined to the hard disk of our personal computer but placed on the servers outside, some of our memory is outside our brains. Like different personal computers store the data on certain some common servers, A (2014, 1), A (2014, 2), B (2014, 10) and others store their memories in the common fields. Like you can access your emails from a common server, A (2014, 1), A (2014,2), B (2014,10) and others have a way of accessing from the common memory bank.

To say there is collective memory is to say that consciousness is connected. A (2014, 1) can change the collective memory by which A (2014, 10) may be affected. The entire network operates on the basis of similarity: a member of species 'A' influences another member of its own species more than a member of species 'B'. Sheldrake calls this principle *morphic resonance*.

J. Krishnamurti[1] once proposed that 10 transformed individuals can make a big impact on the consciousness of mankind. Collective memory and collective consciousness are part of his philosophy – we are not saying that because K said it, it must be true!

The existence of collective memory facilitates collective transformation. Suppose one learns something new, it takes less time for others similarly placed to learn the same. It is found that if crystals are formed out of new substances at one place, at a different place crystal formation out of the same substances takes less time. Time gets reduced as crystallization is repeated.

---

1. From *The Ending of Time*

Studies also showed that if Harvard rats take some time to learn a new technique, Australian rats take less time to learn the same thing! Sheldrake interprets these findings in terms of morphic resonance.

Philosophers as well as scientists debated where the child is in the embryo or where the chicken is in the egg. What is there inside that is giving the final form to life? Sheldrake answers this differently. He says the chicken-related collective memory is shaping the growth of life in the egg. Chicken is not inside the egg – it is not immanent. Chicken is coming from outside – it is transcendent. Man is not evolving from the zygote. He is being nurtured from the zygote by the energy fields outside!

Sheldrake says the human genome project failed to explain in terms of genes the enormous amount of variation because in the first place genes are not the main source of the variation. A huge part of growth is being directed by the external fields.

These connections are not only between an individual life and the collective memory but exist across individual lives too. Sheldrake has done studies to prove that dogs often know when their owners are coming because they have access to their owners' minds! Dogs have a telepathic connection with their owners, he says. How does this take place?

If the minds of A (2014, 1) and A (2014, 2) merged enough, A (2014, 2) will know what goes on A (2014, 1) though not entirely. That is how Sheldrake explains *telepathy*. A mother knows when her child needs milk even when she is not around! She can detect the child's need through certain biological changes in herself! If identical twins are similar in many ways, it may not be only because of similarity of genes but mutual influence also.

Physicists have found that if two previously-related particles (called *entangled particles*) are separated and a change is introduced in one particle, a corresponding change is introduced in the other particle regardless of the distance between the two particles. It shows that increasing the distance between the particles stretches the field instead of separating them. Some such connections exist across the minds entangled. Similarly a family will have a collective mind, treatment of which is beneficial to every member.

Sheldrake's theory can be used even to explain rebirth and karma. You can follow this argument, for it makes an interesting fiction, if not true.

When A (2014, 1) dies in 2060 his brain decays but his memory stored outside does not. And that stored memory guides a zygote and A (2060, 1) is born. That is rebirth. The higher the evolution of memory of A (2014, 1), the better the base with which A (2060, 1) starts his life. So A (2060, 1) is paying for the consequences of his actions during his past birth! That is his karma! Sheldrake's theory fits in well with the Buddhist theory of karma and rebirth, which didn't make use of the concept of God, heaven and hell!

◆ ◆ ◆

Buddha: *Thank you Sheldrake, my ideas on rebirth are not as unscientific as some seem to think.*

Questions to think about

1. Discuss Sheldrake's basic proposals regarding consciousness.
2. Explain morphic resonance.
3. How does Sheldrake explain telepathy?

References

1. *The Moral Philosophers: An Introduction to Ethics* by Richard Norman [This book gave me the basic idea of what ethics is and what can be covered under *Ethical Thought.*]

2. *From Socrates to Sartre, the philosophic quest,* by T.Z. Lavine

3. *The Story of Philosophy* by Will Durant

4. *Emotional Intelligence* by Daniel Goleman

5. *The Divided Self* by R.D. Laing

6. *What The Buddha Taught* by Walpola Sri Rahula

7. *Psychology: An Introduction* by Atkinson and Hilgard

8. BBC documentaries on Nietzsche, Sartre, Muhammad, Jesus Christ and the Buddha.

9. *Self Comes to Mind* by Antonio Damasio

10. *Western Political Thought* by Brian R. Nelson

11. *Science Set Free* by Rupert Sheldrake

12. *Introduction to Political Theory* by John Hoffman and Paul Graham

13. *A History of Political Thought* by Subrata Mukherjee and Sushila Ramaswamy

14. *Peloponnesian War* by Thucydides

Index

Lumbini 119
Lyceum 15

M

Madurai 136
Marshmallow test 172
Martin Heidegger 156
Mary 109
Mary Magdalene 116
Maya 119
Mecca 88
Medina 95
Meenakshi Temple 136
Melian Dialogue 21
midbrain 162
Middle Path 121
Missionaries of Charity 152
morphic resonance 199
Mount Hira 89
MSCEIT 171
Mytilenian Debate 27

N

Nathuram Godse 146
Nazareth 109
Negus 94
Neranjara river 119
nervous system 163
neuron 163
Nicomachean ethics 16
Night Journey 93
nirvana 121
noble morality 54
No Exit 157

O

Odyssey 83

sophists 6
Sparta 1
Suddhodana 119
Sufism 103
Superego 10

T

telepathy 200
thalamus 162
Thrasymachus 6
Thucydides 2
Tiruchuzhi 136
Tiruvannamalai 137

U

Ummah 96
utilitarian approach 46
utility 46

V

Venkataraman Iyer 136

W

Walpola Rahula 124
Walter Mischel 172
What the Buddha Taught 124
will to power 53

Y

Yasodhara 119
Yathrib 95

Z

zakat 101